Portraits
of
Native American Indians

by
Mary Ann Mateo

illustrated by Ted Warren

Cover by Ted Warren

Copyright © Good Apple, 1992

Good Apple
1204 Buchanan St., Box 299
Carthage, IL 62321-0299

SIMON & SCHUSTER *A Paramount Communications Company*

Copyright © Good Apple, 1992

ISBN No. 0-86653-669-8

Printing No. 987654321

Good Apple
1204 Buchanan St., Box 299
Carthage, IL 62321-0299

Table of Contents

GA1322

To the Teacher

The writing process of *Portraits of Native American Indians* has been slow in its completion. When thinking about the topics to be covered and each of the individuals who should be included, I found myself without words on many occasions. What I was experiencing as writer's block was later discovered to be hesitations because of a concern that the book may turn out to be a resource that could foster the typical Indian stereotypes. (This is not the goal of the book.) I wondered how the personalities of the past and the present could be represented without including the age-old stereotypes, which is very possible when one is presenting people of any one particular group. The bias, as it turns out, is that the book not be completed without addressing the issues of stereotypes, which you will find is included in some of the activities.

As we look at the title, *Portraits of Native American Indians*, it is important to note that there are some people who dislike being referred to as "Native Americans" and some who are equally uncomfortable with the use of "Indian." In a more recent movement the term "Indigenous People" is being used, as well as "Native People." It must be clarified that this book title includes originally known tribal people of North America, mainly those who are native to the areas of the United States. It is not intended to be disrespectful toward nor insensitive to any group, tribe or individual.

It is most important that each person be recognized by his own tribal affiliation. In most culturally similar groups, many individuals tend to appreciate recognition according to their specific cultural heritage (for example, Mexican, Cuban, Puerto Rican vs. Hispanic, Latino or Chinese, Japanese, East Indian vs. Orientals, Asians). Here is a true story about a small child in a kindergarten class, who was being taunted by other children who were calling her "Indian." She responded with a definite tone in her voice that she was not an "Indian." The teacher overheard the incident and later asked the child what she thought she was if she was not an Indian. The child proudly replied, "I'm a Navajo." This child's answer seemed to reflect a sense of belonging and certainly a real pride in tribe, clan and family. The use of "Native American Indian" throughout this book is quite general in meaning. There are many tribal nations that this title represents and hopefully most tribes will be included and/or represented.

Because of circumstances of the times and the environments, many of the tribal people have oral histories. Since most of the Native People's languages were not written until within the past one hundred years, there is little documentation that reflects their personal historical perspectives. Through the years it has been a tradition for the elders of the tribes to pass their history on through an oral process. The elders would repeatedly tell their stories to the young until they were learned and then the stories would be told again and again, from one generation to the next.

Hopefully the student will learn about the people, the culture, the history and himself through the reading and the activities included in this book.

Part One: Native American Indians

Who Are Native American Indians?

Some anthropologists say that there was an unknown number of Native American Indians who existed and lived in the Americas for about 70,000 years. No one really knows how many tribes actually lived on this land called *America*. Through the era of the Pre-Columbian Indian Societies, some of these tribes vanished with no trace nor reason for their disappearance.

There are several theories regarding where Native American Indian people actually came from. No one is absolutely sure of their exact origins. It is said that the Eskimos, Apache and Navajos came to the North American continent over the Bering Strait, which was once a land bridge that connected the areas known as Siberia and Alaska. Other theories state that some tribal people traveled from South and Central America to the northern area of the continent.

This book will focus on some individuals and other information regarding the Native American Indian people from the turn of the nineteenth century and through the turn of the twenty-first century.

In the 1400's the Native American Indian people began their experiences of conflicts of warfare and compromises between themselves and the non-Indians who had invaded their land. These invaders came from other lands of the earth. It is said that during this time there were 10 to 12 million Native American Indians living on this land known as the United States of America, which does not include Hawaii and Alaska. There were different tribal nations with many different cultures, beliefs and languages. During the next four hundred years, an unknown number of these people were destroyed. The destructions were caused by many epidemic diseases, which were brought over by the Europeans, and wars that took place with the same foreign invaders. Some of the tribes were completely destroyed with not one member left to survive.

By 1881 there were only one quarter of a million Native people left to carry on their traditions, their values and their history. Many of these people had their land taken from them; they were forced away from their homes and left with very little of what was once theirs. Those who did survive had to adapt to the new changes and make every effort they could to mend what was left of their cultures and to keep their traditional values alive.

Almost two hundred years have passed since that time, and there are still negotiations taking place today between the Native American nations and the United States government. There are still those who are working very hard to keep their cultural traditions and values as they once were.

Today there are 350 tribes that are recognized by the U.S. government and do not include the unrecognized tribes in California. These tribes are collectively thought of as Native American Indians. It would be impossible to introduce all of them in detail in this writing. This book will only be able to introduce you to a limited number of individuals from a few tribes and may not include all the various tribal nations. If you were to study each of these cultures that existed before and exist today, it would probably take many years to learn about all of them. You may want to study each of the tribal nations in more detail on your own.

GA1322

Activities

What Would You Do?

Take time to think about what you have just read. Think about what you might do if some group of people came into your neighborhood and home and told you that you and your family could no longer live in your home nor in its land. This home is familiar to you with all of its happy and sad moments. These strange people seem to think they know what is best for you. They tell you of another place that you could live, a place of their choice and not the choice of you or your family. They do this because they want to live in your home, and they want the gold and other riches that are buried on your land.

Write or discuss the following: How would you feel if this happened to you? What would you do about it?

Creating a Scenario

After thinking and talking about what you might do in this kind of a situation, get together as a group and create a play that reflects what you might do. Create your players and the roles they will portray. Write down the words you agree people might say, the things they might do and also what could happen. Present this play in front of the class (or even for your parents).

If this is done in several groups, and after all plays are presented, take time to discuss with each other the solutions that each group came up with and what might work or what might not work and why?

GA1322

My Home Culture Activity

You each have a home culture. Your family has their own beliefs, values, customs, language and life-style.

1. Ask your parents if you are not sure what these are before you talk about this with your classmates.

2. Collect pictures of you and your family spending time together, eating, working and playing. Get pictures of your house, pets, favorite places in your home, favorite things and important events. Put these into a book and below each write what is in the picture. If photographs are not available, draw your pictures.

3. Share these books with your class and take time to talk about the differences and similarities you have in common.

Your teacher may choose to do some activities that have to do with what you have in your culture book so that others in your class might better understand your traditional family customs.

Research the Bering Strait

Do some research on the Bering Strait and find out all the information you can about this formation and its geological history. This is very interesting information for you to write a report about and/or make a topographical map which shows how it was and how it is now.

Research the Ancient Tribes of North America

You might want to do some research on the ancient tribes that existed on the northern continent of the Americas hundreds of years ago. What can you find out about these people? How did they live? What did they eat? How did they dress? What was the environment like at the time? As you study this you will probably come up with many more questions.

To the Student
The Tribal People and Their Land

The title *Native American Indians* is being used in this book to represent a group of people who share many similarities and also have differences. In the past these people have been referred to as Indians. Today there are those who prefer "Native People," while there are some who are also using the term "Indigenous People."

These people are members of different tribal nations. The people of these individual nations have traditionally valued the lives of each and every individual, the family unit, the clan, the tribal nation and the tribal people as a whole.

Here is a true story that conveys the importance of belonging to a particular tribal nation. A few years ago a teacher was teaching a kindergarten class at a reservation school. She found one of her students was in distress because of being teased by some children. The teacher overheard the child say in an angry tone of voice, "I am not an Indian!" The teacher approached and comforted her and asked the child what she thought she was. The child responded, "I'm a Navajo." This child's answer was accurate. The story shows that, even at this young age, most people like to be described as correctly as possible. The story may also convey that the child could also have a negative idea of what represents an Indian. But without further information we can only guess that she was reacting to the stereotype, which she may have learned from watching movies.

What is a stereotype? According to a definition given in the book *Unlearning "Indian" Stereotypes*, a stereotype is "an oversimplified generalization about a particular group, race or sex, which usually carries derogatory implications." This means that one characterization or description may be the same for the entire group of people. For example, for years all Native American Indians were thought to wear feathers in their hair or live in teepees. These statements are not completely true because the tribal nations of the Plains wore the feather headdresses and lived in teepees. Not *all* people of *all* tribal nations wore feathers in their hair nor lived in teepees. You might want your teacher to give you more information about what a stereotype is. There are some excellent resource books available.

It would be important when studying the different tribal nations to talk about the differences and the similarities, as well as their differences and similarities of the past and present. (For example, feather headdresses are used for special ceremonies and dances and are not something one might see as an everyday occurrence.)

4

GA1322

Since there are so many tribal nations in the United States, it would be impossible to include each of them in much detail in this book, but we will cover some individuals and refer to each by their tribal affiliation.

Many of the tribal nations originally lived in different areas of the country and were later assigned reservation land by the U.S. government. Although there is reservation land, many of the people have chosen to move to different areas of the U.S. continent. Some often return to visit friends and family.

GA1322

Here is a listing of some of the tribal nations.

Abenaki

Apache: Chirocahua

         Coyotero

         Mimbreno

Arapaho

Bannock

Blackfoot

Catawba

Cayuse

Cherokee

Cheyenne

Chinook

Chippewa

Choctaw

Comanche

Cree

Creek

Crow

Delaware

Eskimo

Fox

Haida

Hawaiian

Iroquois: Cayuga

         Mohawk

         Onedia

         Onondaga

         Seneca

         Tuscarora

Kalispel

Kansa

Kawia

Kickapoo

Kiowa

Kwakiutl

Luiseno

Mahican

Mandan

Menominee

Miami

Miccosukee

Modoc

Mohave

Mohegan

Montauk

Narragansett

Navajo

Nez Perce

Niantic

Ojibwa

Omaha

Osage

Ottawa

Paiute

Pamunkey

Pautuxet

Pawnee

Pemaquid

Pequot

Pima

Pocasset

Ponca

Potawatomi

Powhatan

Pueblo: Acoma

         Cochiti

         Hopi

         Isleta

         Laguna

         San Ildefonso

         San Juan

         Santa Domingo

         Santa Clara

         Taos

         Zuni

Salish: Duwamish

         Sinkiuse

         Spokane

Sauk

Seminole

Shawnee

Shoshoni

Sioux: Brule

         Hunkpapa

         Mdewakanton

         Meniconjon

         Oglala

         Santee

         Teton

         Wahpekuti

         Wahpeton

         Yankton

         Yanktonal

Tionantati

Tlingit

Ute

Wampanoag

Wanapum

Washo

Winnebago

Yaki

Yakima

Yavapai

As you can see there are many tribes listed. Many of these names may also be familiar to you.

Activities

Familiar Names

Of the names listed, how many have you heard of before? Make a list of those. Where have you heard them before? If you hear the name, what do you usually think of?

Research a Tribe

Choose one tribe that you are most interested in and gather information that you can share with the rest of your class.

GA1322

There are ten geographical areas where Native American Indians have historically lived and may still live today. These areas include:

1. Alaska
2. California
3. Eastern Woodlands
4. Great Basin
5. Hawaii
6. Northwest Coast
7. Plains
8. Plateau Region
9. Southeast
10. Southwest

You probably recognize some of the areas, especially Alaska, California and Hawaii. The other areas mentioned include states as well. You may want to research these areas to find out what states are included in these areas and what tribal nations are from these areas.

Research Activity

In groups, select one of the geographical areas. Go to your school or county library and find out how much you can learn about these areas and the Native Americans that live or lived on this land. Here are some questions to help you with your research. Add your own questions to the list.

Where is the area located on a map?
What states does this area include?
What tribal nations actually may have lived there and which still do?

When you have found out as much as you can, figure out a way in which you as a group can present your findings to the rest of the class. After all the groups have presented, discuss what you found to be most interesting and why. What would you like to know more about?

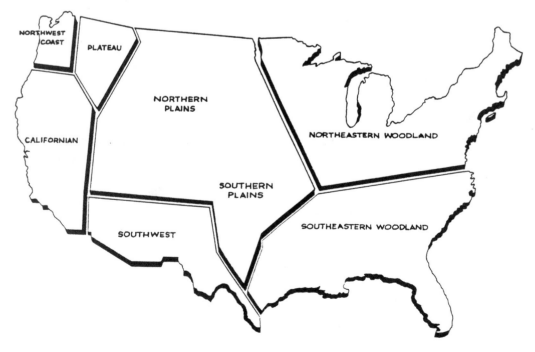

8

GA1322

When you look at the names of the states, you will find that many of them have origins of some Native American languages. The Office of Anthropology of the Smithsonian Institution has compiled a listing of these names.

Alabama	Believed to mean "here we rest," Creek by origin
Alaska	A French interpretation of a Sioux word and a form of the word *Kansas*
Connecticut	Mohican, from the word *KwEnhtEkot*, meaning "long river place"
Hawaii	Hawaiian, from the older form of the word *Kawayi* which meant "homeland"
Idaho	Shoshone, named for an Indian tribe; *Ida* which means "salmon" and *ho* which means "eaters"
Illinois	French version of the word *Illni*, meaning "man or warrior" and referring to a seventeenth century confederation of tribes living in the Illinois River Valley
Iowa	Sioux, *Ayuxwa*, meaning "one who puts to sleep"
Kansas	Comes from the Wyandot Iroquois word for *Plain*, referring to land, now part of central Kentucky
Massachusetts	Algonquian, named for Massachusetts Indians, meaning "large hill place" and referring to Great Blue Hill, which can be seen from Boston Harbor
Michigan	Chippewa, probably from the word *majiigan* that means "clearing"
Minnesota	Dakota Sioux, from the word *Mnishota*, meaning "milky" or "clouded water"
Mississippi	Chippewa or Choctaw, meaning "large river"
Missouri	Algonquian, named after an Indian tribe of that area, meaning "canoe haver"
Nebraska	Omaha, from Niboapka, meaning "broad water" and referring to the Platte River
New Mexico	Named because it borders on Mexico. Its name is from the Aztec word for gold, *Mecitii*.
North and South Dakota	Sioux, the word *dakohta* meaning "friend"
Ohio	Iroquios could mean "beautiful" or referring to any large river
Oklahoma	Meaning "red people"
Tennessee	From the Cherokee word *Tanasi*, meaning "unknown"
Texas	Spanish adaption of Caddo word *teysha*, meaning "hello, friend"
Utah	Apache, from *Yuttahih* meaning "one that is higher up," referring to the Ute people who lived higher in the mountain country than the Navajo or Apache of the area
Wisconsin	Chippewa, from *miskonsin* meaning "grassy place." Was interpreted by the French as Ouisconsin and later changed to *Wisconsin*.
Wyoming	Delaware, meaning "large prairie place"

 GA1322

Native American Language Search

Study a map of the state you live in and see if you can find names of places that might have originated from a Native American language. Make a list of the names of the places you have found. Look for these names in a dictionary or in the encyclopedia to see if the names do originate from a native language.

Using a blank map of your state, write in all the names you have found in their appropriate areas.

Memory Activity

After reviewing the list of the many different tribal nations, take some time to see if you can remember the names that were listed.

On a separate piece of paper write down all the tribal names you can remember, without peeking! (Do not worry about spelling.)

How many did you remember? _____

Write down all the names you remembered below, and this time you can use your book to find the correct spellings.

_____

_____

_____

_____

_____

_____

_____

_____

Learning About a Tribal Nation

Choose a tribal nation that you did not list that you are interested in learning about. See if you can find something that is written about that nation.

Name of tribal nation: _____

Names of books where information is found:

_____

_____

In what state does this tribal nation live? _____

Is this the original state they lived in before the time of reservation land?   Yes   No

Does this nation now live on a reservation?   Yes   No

Are they located in the same state as before?   Yes   No

Looking at a topographical map, compare the area where they lived to where their reservation is now. Do you find that there is a difference?

Write about the difference and how you think the tribal nation felt about the change.

_____

_____

What other information did you learn about this tribal nation?

_____

_____

_____

_____

_____

_____

_____

_____

_____

_____

_____

_____

_____

_____

11

GA1322

Easy Word Search

Hidden in this word search are tribal names and other words that refer to the Southwest area of the United States. See if you can find them all. Circle the ones you find.

```
S E N D E Y E S H O S H O N I C E T
A V I D N A V A J O P E R I L L E A
N O T U R Q U P I E S A C O M A D O
T H I S T U P A S S O P O L L D U S
A C H O P I N C O A L I L Y Z U N I
D O C A V E E H C N E L O A N N E W
O S O U T H W E S T O U R E A A L F
M U C T H E M I N A U T A H A B L E
I T C E N T E D I C O A D U D A Y J
N I N E T E X O K L A H O M A L E E
G O O D Y B I L T A M U D I V Y E M
O V D E E Z C U R R C H E Y E N N E
N A A R I Z O N A A L M O N N U T Z
```

Acoma	Colorado	Oklahoma	Taos
Apache	Hopi	Santa Clara	Utah
Arizona	Jemez	Santa Domingo	Ute
Cheyenne	Navajo	Shoshoni	Yaqui
Cochiti	New Mexico	Southwest	

12

GA1322

Hard Word Search

Circle the words in this puzzle and see how many of the hidden tribal names you can find. They may be across, up or down, backwards or even diagonal. Have fun.

```
N A T I V E A M E R I C A N I N D I A N S
E C H O M I A M I N N R L E M E O D N E H
Z H I W I N R A N D D E O T T A W A L S O
P I M A L D A T E D T E N D O N T H E S S
O T A L L A P A C H E K E Y D E L A Y A H
J O H A R D A N C E S T E A M Z I M I N O
I E C R O P H O E S K I C K A P O O P E N
B L A C K F O O T L I C K I C E E H O P I
W I N R D R A W I N M T O M C R A E T U E
A C B E E N I P S I O U X A R C H G T E X
T F E E L A V A N E D I N E D E X A A B S
E M O H A V E T S M O I N S E M I N O L E
R O T X W A T C O H C H I N O O K S T O P
B O X O A J O S X O S F E E M A H I C A N
E A R C R O W I N N E B A G O T X E K I L
E X I T E N D U E F I D D L Y A V A P A I
```

Apache
Arapaho
Blackfoot
Chinook
Choctaw
Cree
Creek
Crow
Delaware
Eskimo
Fox

Hopi
Kickapoo
Mahican
Miami
Modoc
Mohave
Mohegan
Native American Indians
Navajo
Nez Percé
Ojibwa
Omaha

Ottawa
Pima
Pueblo
Seminole
Shoshoni
Sioux
Ute
Yakima
Yavapai
Winnebago

13

Oral and Pictoral History

When studying the history of people, we often rely upon what is written in our history books. As you study the Native American Indian history, it is important to realize that each tribal nation has a history of its own. Although you may find many books written today, some of these histories may not always be complete or may be written by non-Indians and possibly with a biased perspective, which may mean a history that is not perceived from the eyes and heart of a Native American Indian. Most tribal histories were traditional stories that have been told either orally or pictorally. This was done mainly because Native American Indian languages had not had a written system until within the past hundred years.

Sequoya
(Cherokee)
1776-1843

For the northern Native American Indians, the beginning of the written language was started by Sequoya, the son of Wurteh, a Cherokee woman and a daughter of a chief. Sequoya developed an alphabet writing system. When he first introduced his system to the tribe, the people thought he was practicing witchcraft and his home and the papers were burned. Sequoya left and settled with other Cherokees who had moved to Arkansas. He continued his work on the system. After twelve years he was able to convince the tribe that this system was valuable to the tribal people. Sequoya's system was formally accepted and adopted by the Cherokee Tribal Council in 1821. This was the first Indian writing system north of Mexico and has proved to be a great achievement in Cherokee education as well as the possibility of developing other Indian languages into writing systems.

Today, especially in many tribal schools, you can find books written in the native languages that are used in teaching the young. The tribes have recognized the importance of keeping the languages alive and thereby wanting the children to have the skills to speak, read and write their language. Many of the traditional native stories have also been written in English so that English speakers may learn and understand. Many of these stories include animals as the main characters, humor and will usually have a traditional value or moral to be learned.

Most oral histories are the stories that the tribal elders, the oldest members of the tribe and mostly grandparents, shared with the younger children. The children would listen to these stories over and over, asking questions and learning until they knew the stories by heart. The stories told were mostly fable in nature and had important messages of morals, values and beliefs of the tribe's traditional heritage. The stories were often told in this way so that children would be able to understand the messages, much like the stories or fairy tales that you may have heard or read growing up.

Another way of telling a story of an event would be to draw pictures, which was a system that the Egyptians used many years ago. You may find pictures drawn on cave walls or rocks in different areas of the United States. Because most of the pictoral documents were destroyed in warfare or lost, there are only a few that exist today in museums and within the tribal nations themselves. Most of these documented events may have been drawn on tanned hides, woven material or even paper if available. The following are some examples.

Dakota Winters Calendar
Lone Dog (Dakota Sioux)
Lone Dog recorded on a buffalo robe drawings showing the events that took place from 1800 to 1871, which is a Dakota custom. He begins his drawings in the center of the hide and moves in a spiral counterclockwise.

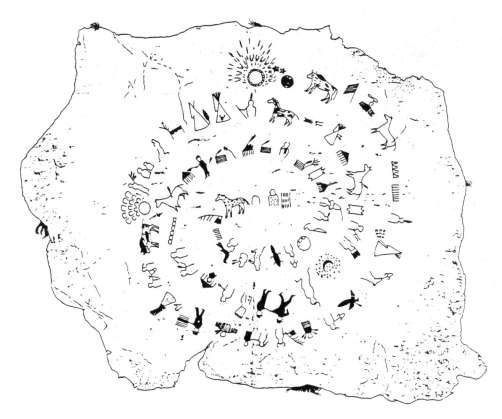

Pictoral Recording of the Battle of Little Big Horn

Kicking Bear (Sioux)

Kicking Bear was a survivor of the Battle of Little Big Horn, in Montana in 1876. Twenty-two years later he painted his recollection of that battle on muslin. This pictograph is now in the Southwest Museum in Los Angeles.

Red Horse (Sioux)

A pictoral recording of the battle at Little Big Horn (the Greasy Grass River), which took place in June of 1876, was drawn by Red Horse, a Sioux chief who was a participant in the battle. Five years after the battle, Red Horse told his story to Dr. Charles McChesney, who persuaded him to draw the pictures. On forty-one sheets of paper, Red Horse drew the events before and through the end of the battle. The U.S. Army surgeon translated the sign language into English.

GA1322

Activities

A Writing System

In small groups develop a writing system of your own. Make up your own symbols to represent an alphabet and words that you think are important. Taking these symbols, use them to write a story. After this is completed, share copies of your story with other groups and see if they can figure out what your group wrote about. Before sharing what the story is about, pick someone in each group to read the story to everyone and see if reading the story helps others to better understand what has actually been written. See how close others may come to understanding your group's writing system. This activity may take several days.

17

GA1322

My Family History

Materials:

cassette tape recorder or videotape recorder
tablet
pencil for notes

Ask an elder in your family if you may interview him/her about the family history. This person you interview may be a great grandparent, grandparent, aunt, uncle or possibly a parent. Make an appointment to set aside an hour or more for this interview. Before meeting with this person, write down a list of questions you want to ask. You may also want to use a tape recorder or videotape recorder during the interview.

Here is a list of some questions you might want to ask and add some of your own. You may also want to give your list to the person before your interview so that he/she may have time to think about the questions and gather pictures and other things to share with you.

Sample Questions:

1. Where did our family ancestors come from?
2. When did they come here? Where did they settle first?
3. What made them move, if they moved?
4. What did the different people do to make a living?
5. What is known about different individuals?

Taking the information that was shared with you, what did you learn about your family history? Write about what you have learned. You may also want to share what you learned with your classmates.

It might also be more interesting to interview an elder from both of your parents' families so that what you learn about your family history is more complete.

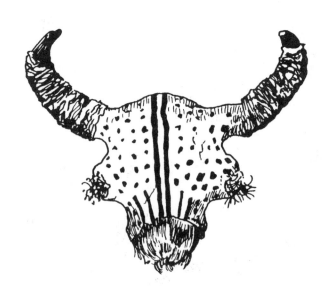

GA1322

Spiral Pictoral Calendar

Materials:

construction paper, butcher paper or tagboard (Materials such as muslin or a chamois may be something to consider using.)
paints
India ink
colored markers or pencils

Taking the information you learned from the interviews, draw pictures beginning with the earliest event that you learned about. Starting in the middle of a large piece of paper or tagboard, draw a symbol that represents each event that you feel has importance to your family history. Continue drawing your pictures in a spiral until you come to the present time. You may also want to make a listing of the pictures and their meanings on your calendar. These would make a nice class display.

To further this activity, you may make copies of your calendar and the listing and put them in a time capsule as a class or individually. Bury the time capsule somewhere to be dug up at a later time.

You may want to frame your original spiral calendar and give it to someone in your family.

Unframed you could make a calendar just by attaching a yearly calendar to the drawing itself. This would certainly make a wonderful gift.

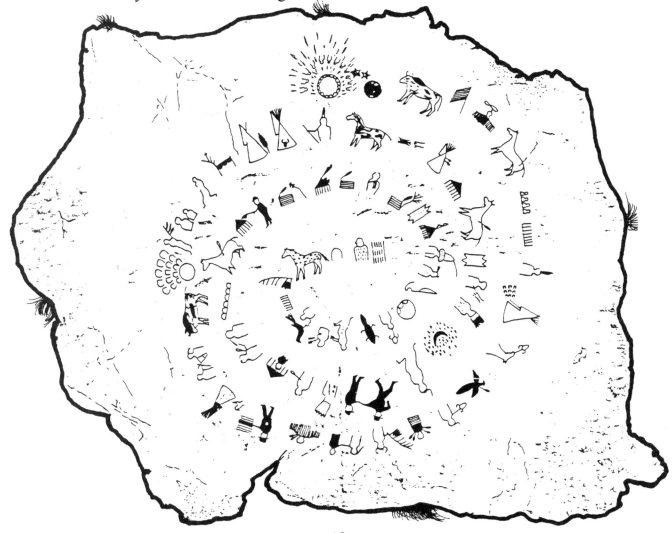

19

GA1322

Personal Pictoral History Book

Materials:

paper
drawing tools
cardboard
glue
adhesive Con-Tact, shelf lining or material scraps
book binding tape

Let's make a special book all about you. Now think about your life from the time you were born until today. Take some pieces of paper and draw pictures of the important events of your life. Make sure you leave some space on the left side of your drawing for the book binding. You may want to write something under each of the pictures to tell what the picture is about. Take all of your pictures and arrange them in order, starting from your birth and ending with the present.

Book Cover

1. Measure the size of the paper you have drawn your pictures on.

2. Cut two pieces of cardboard so that they are ½" (1.25 cm) wider and 1" (2.54 cm) longer than your finished pages.

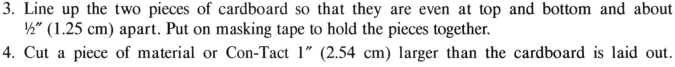

3. Line up the two pieces of cardboard so that they are even at top and bottom and about ½" (1.25 cm) apart. Put on masking tape to hold the pieces together.

4. Cut a piece of material or Con-Tact 1" (2.54 cm) larger than the cardboard is laid out.

5. If you are using Con-Tact paper, peel back half of the paper and put half of the cardboard on the sticky side. Then finish peeling the rest of the Con-Tact and put the other half of cardboard on. Fold over the corners first onto the cardboard. Next fold the sides over and then the top edges.

   When using material, apply glue evenly on the cardboard opposite of masking tape side, one side at a time. Apply glue to the overlapping sides of the material and fold over to cover edge of cardboard.

6. Cut Con-Tact paper or material to cover inside of the cardboard. Peel Con-Tact back and apply. Or apply glue to inside of cardboard and place material on glued area making sure the edges of the material are folded under for a more finished look. (Make sure everything is dry before continuing on.)

7. Sew or staple finished pages together. You may want to include a heading page and an extra page at the end.

8. Tape the front and back of finished pages to the inside of the front and back covers with binding.

Enjoy reading each other's history!

GA1322

Writing a Tale

Think about what a moral or a value is. Together as a class make a list of the different kinds of morals or values that you know about. From the list you make together, select one you will use to write your own story that will convey the meaning of the moral you have chosen. Start your tale with "Once upon a time . . . ." When the stories are finished, everyone will take time to share his tale with the rest of the class. After each has been read, the class will then try to guess what the moral of the story is.

Another activity is to choose the best story to present in the form of a play to the class, with the author of the story as the one who will direct the play.

21

GA1322

Native American Indian Housing

Years ago Native American Indians lived in many different forms of housing. Huts, cliff dwellings and round structures made of sod were a few of those forms. Native American Indians have lived in basic modern houses for many years now. For some families their homes have no electricity or plumbing because of the remote location of the land. On some of the reservations simple houses with running water and electricity are built by the government agency HUD (Housing and Urban Development). Here are a few traditional housing forms of different Native American Indian tribal groups.

Tipi

Even today, when people think of Native American Indian life, an image of the tipi comes to mind. For the Dakota Sioux, the word *tipi* means "used for dwelling." Other written spellings of this word are *teepee* and *tepee*.

A tipi is a cone-shaped structure that was used as portable housing, mostly by the Plains Indians, because they traveled from place to place, according to the seasons and the needs of the people. The tipi was not only useful and portable, it was also easy to assemble, taking only two people to put it together.

A tipi was made by placing three main poles, 18 to 20 feet (5.4 to 6 m) in length, in a tripod position and then adding twelve or more poles, which formed the ribs that support the outside covering. The lodge covering was usually made of dressed buffalo hides. Designs of the covering differed from tribe to tribe. The bottom edge of the covering was braced to the ground using wooden pegs. Smoke flaps at the top of the tipi were used to let smoke rise, and the poles connected to these flaps would be moved according to the direction of the wind. In case of rain or snow, the flaps could also be closed to cover the opening. The doorway into the tipi was also made of the same or similar material which could be pulled out of the way for entry. The inside was about 15 feet (4.5 m) across the floor, which was plenty of room for beds and other items.

GA1322

Although the tipi is not commonly used as permanent housing today, it is used as portable housing for special gatherings and tribal ceremonies. Because of the extinction of the once huge herds of buffalo, today the outer coverings of tipis may be made out of tanned cowhides or may be waterproof muslin.

Clustered Housing

Ramada or Pueblo

Other types of traditional housing include the ramada, an apartment-like adobe dwelling, which is often referred to as a pueblo or clustered housing. This type of housing is very much like many apartment houses that are seen in cities. Apartment living is not a new idea. This form of dwelling place for the Native American Indian goes back to the days of the Anasazi (The Old Ones) hundreds of years ago. Old ruins of these dwellings can be seen today in the southwest areas of Arizona, New Mexico and Colorado.

Today the Hopi and Acoma people, as well as many other pueblo communities, choose to live in pueblos. The Acoma Pueblo, also known as Sky City, is the oldest "inhabited" pueblo in North America. The Zuni people also choose to build their modern homes so closely together that they too look like apartments.

Not all Native American Indians feel comfortable living in clustered style housing. Some enjoy the privacy of scattered housing. This is certainly true for the Navajo. If there are a few homes on one particular piece of land, the other homes belong to close relatives and they are not built close to the others, as in clustered housing.

GA1322

Hogan

Many Navajo families live in a house which is called a hogan. Traditionally hogans may have been built with nine, eight or even seven sides. Today the hogan is like a hexagon in shape. This six-sided house is made of layered logs and filled in between with a mixture of earth and grasses. The main door into a hogan traditionally faces the east. Located in the center of the roof made of posts and mud mixture is a smoke hole. Some of the newer hogan roofs are made of modern materials and may have one or two windows. A wood stove is located on the floor in the center, which is important for ceremonial purposes, as well as heating.

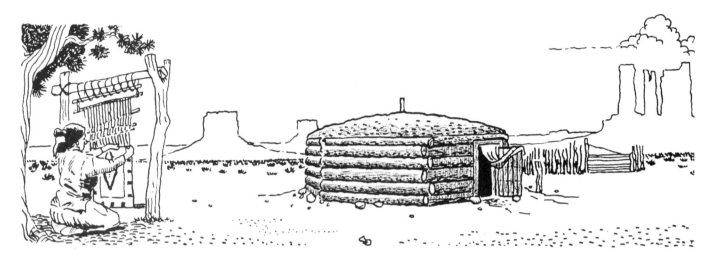

A Navajo family may live in a modern home and also have a hogan on their property for ceremonial purposes. The hogan is not just a house; there are special traditional reasons for why and how the hogan is built.

Chickee

Because of the hot climate and frequent floods in the Florida Everglades, many of the Miccosukee people choose to build and live in chickees today.

GA1322

A chickee frame is made of strong cypress poles anchored deep into the ground. The floors of the chickee are built at least three feet (.9 m) off the ground with smaller poles and is almost tablelike since it is not attached to the basic frame of the chickee. The reason the floors are so high is for protection from dampness, flooding and snakes. There are no walls built on the chickee, providing a constant fresh air flow. The thatched roofs are made with a covering of many palmetto fronds that are layered and hang low over the sides of the main frame much like a curtain. These fronds help to keep any rain from falling through to the inside and protect the items stored in the rafters just under the roof.

A Miccosukee clan camp may have several chickees, and they are shared by the people living in that same compound. Individual chickees, may be used for different purposes. Each family has its own living and sleeping chickees, and then there is one main chickee located in the center of the others that is used as a cooking area where the women prepare the meals for the clan. Chickees may also be used for areas of craft making and storage.

U-Ma-Cha

Somewhat like a teepee, the u-ma-cha was a dwelling used by the Yosemite of California. It was made by first placing a few poles ten or twelve feet (3 or 3.6 m) long into the ground covering an area of about twelve feet (3.6 m). The tops of the poles fit closely together at the top, leaving an open area for smoke to escape from the fire burning in the center. Cedar bark was used as the outside covering and a portable door covered the south entrance. During the summer season, the u-ma-cha was used as a storage house and the people would use brush arbors which were cooler.

GA1322

Activities

As you can see there are several types of housing used by Native American Indians. See if you can find information about other dwellings not mentioned.

Miniature Housing Models

Select one of the different types of Native American housing and gather building information and the materials that would be best to make the housing you choose. (You may want to find books that have illustrations of how the particular housing is made.)

Build the model or models of your housing. If you happen to make several of the same kind, you may want to create a small scene using the models and pieces of shrubs for plants and whatever else you would like to include.

Making a Tipi

Here is a diagram for making a tipi. You may want to have the diagram enlarged to make it easier to handle.

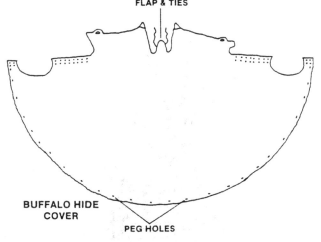

Using paper, trace the diagram and cut it out. Long toothpicks, swab sticks or wooden skewers can be used as poles for the tipi. Use three of the wooden sticks to make the tripod base of the tipi. Connect them at the top with a string. Then add the other sticks to form a cone-shaped rib structure.

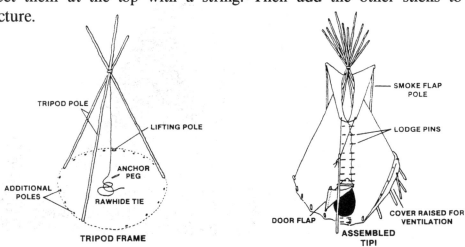

Now add the paper covering to the outside of the poles.

This activity will help you to better understand the building of the tipi.

You might want to paint decorations on the outside of the paper covering with pictures of things that are important to you. This may be easier to do before attaching it to the poles.

Connect the straight edges of the covering with straight pins to make the front of the tipi. The door flap covering should be a little larger than the opening itself.

Class Tipi Project

If you have the resources to obtain the materials to make a large tipi, this could be a great class project for older children.

Find detailed instructions on how to build a tipi. You will need a large area of at least 20 x 20 feet (6 x 6 m) to erect the tipi.

As with most building activities, there are many math problems to solve with the making of a large tipi.

Class teams could be assigned different tasks to complete this activity.

GA1322

Mix and Match

Using your pencil, draw a line from the type of housing to the tribal group that uses or has used the housing.

Tipi   Yosemite

Hogan   Miccosukee

Pueblo   Plains Indians

Chickee   Navajo

U-Ma-Cha   Hopi

28   GA1322

Part Two: Portraits of the Nineteenth Century

The Leaders

Chief Joseph
or Hinmatowyalahtqit
(Nez Percé)
1832-1904

Chief Joseph is one of the most well-known Indian leaders of the nineteenth century. He was a peace-loving man, but as history has shown he and his people were forced into war because they did not want to give up their land where they had lived in peace for years. After many battles, Chief Joseph knew that the only way the war could end would be either an annihilation of his people, surrender or retreat. Because most of the people left were elders, women and children, Chief Joseph decided to leave the land and move to Canada where he felt everyone would be safe.

After traveling 1500 miles (2415 km) over four states, the last battle was fought at **Bear Paws**, Montana, only forty miles (64.40 km) from the Canadian border. Just a few of his people were able to get away and find their way to Canada before this final battle took place. On October 5, 1887, with only a small number left of those who stayed behind to fight, Chief Joseph surrendered.

GA1322

After the battle at Bear Paws, Chief Joseph spoke. The words he spoke have been heard and read by many since that day. Here is an important part of that speech in 1887.

"I am tired of fighting. Our chiefs are killed. . . . It is cold and we have no blankets. The little children are freezing to death. I want time to look for my children and see how many I can find. Maybe I shall find them among the dead. Hear me my Chiefs; I am tired, my heart is sick and sad. From where the sun now stands, I will fight no more forever."

As history shows, he no longer fought the battles of war, but he did continue to stand for and work toward the welfare of his people. He held on to a dream that he and his people would be allowed to return to the Wallowa Valley, the place that was once their home. Some were sent to the Lapwai Reservation in Idaho in 1885. Chief Joseph and some others were sent to the Colville Reservation in the state of Washington, where Chief Joseph later died in 1904.

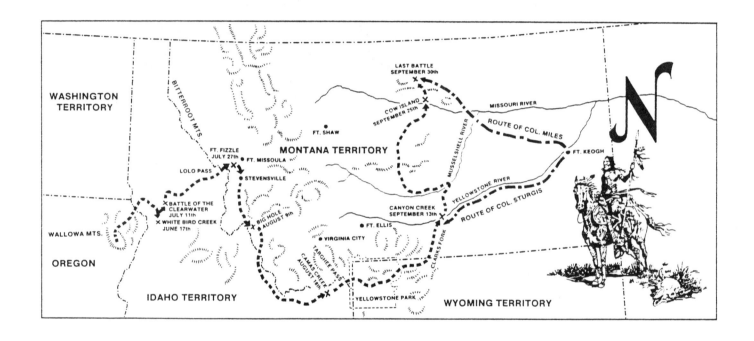

Red Cloud
Mahpiya Luta
(Oglala Sioux)
1822-1909

Because of his many skills and bravery, Red Cloud was selected to be a chief, a right that is usually inherited. His name was given to him by Chief Man Afraid of His Horses because of an approach he used in a skirmish with the Cheyenne and Arapaho, where his idea of the attack was to each be wrapped with red blankets. And so, with the victory came the name Red Cloud. His intelligence and bravery was proven many times over. He was well-respected by the people of the tribe and others.

Red Cloud fought long and hard for the land he and his people had lived and hunted on. He wanted to defend what he felt were the Indians' last hunting grounds. The U.S. government wanted gold and expansion. The Indians wanted to keep their hunting grounds.

With dedication to his cause and his people, Red Cloud continually refused to speak to government officials until he had his demands met. He wanted to get all the people who had invaded the area off the land on the Bozeman Trail. It was not until Fort Phil Kearney and Fort Reno stood empty that Red Cloud kept his promise.

In November 1868, Red Cloud went to Fort Laramie and there he signed a new treaty. He also vowed that he would never again war against the United States government. He kept his word even when the U.S. government did not. Even though he did not fight battles of war, he kept on fighting the governmental system by speaking for the rights of his people. Red Cloud traveled to Washington, D.C., several times to defend those rights.

Red Cloud became a well-respected chief and is remembered well by his people. Red Cloud lived at the Pine Ridge Reservation in South Dakota until his death on December 10, 1909. At his death he had become angry, disillusioned, betrayed, blind and ill.

GA1322

Crazy Horse
Tashunka Witka
(Brule-Oglala Sioux)
1841-1877

Crazy Horse is thought of by many Native American Indians as the greatest of the Sioux leaders. He was the son of Spotted Tail's sister and an Oglala medicine man. His father taught him the ways of the medicine man, and he had the gifts which earned him the right to be a powerful medicine man.

Whenever he went into battle, he wore a smooth stone behind his ear, his hair loose and flowing with a red hawk feather tied to it. He had seen himself this way in a dream riding a very unusual horse. It is said that this dream was a vision of good medicine. The talisman was his protection. He rode and fought in many battles. He took many dangerous chances, and he was never wounded in battle.

After fighting many battles, he was found surrendering in a group of about one thousand other Indians on May 6, 1877. They were promised reservation land. Crazy Horse did not like living on the reservation. He was a free spirit who wanted to roam the lands he was familiar with.

He decided to leave the reservation and wanted to go to Yellowstone with a scout but instead went to the Spotted Tail Agency where he was followed and captured by Captain Clark and his Indian scouts. Instead of being taken back to his people and the reservation, he was taken to a stockade. When Crazy Horse realized he was to be jailed, he tried to escape. It was during this time he was stabbed with a bayonet by a soldier. This was how he met his death on September 7, 1877. His last request was that his parents return his heart back to the land of his birth. This request was honored, and his parents took his body for burial. Some say that the body of the great Oglala warrior is buried somewhere near Wounded Knee.

GA1322

Activities

The Nez Percé traveled nearly 1700 miles (2737 km), which took them 108 days. They crossed four territories, what we call states today.

Using a copy of a United States map, trace the route that was taken and where they fought. When you have completed this, you will have learned what territories the Nez Percé crossed and the conditions of the terrain they traveled.

Map the Journey of the Nez Percé

Beginning in the northwest area of the United States, the Nez Percé began their journey. They traveled from the Wallowa Mountains to White Bird Creek (June 17). They fought the battle at Clearwater on July 11. After this battle they headed northeast through Lolo Pass and to Fort Fizzle (July 27), not far from Fort Missoula. Then they traveled south through Stevensville and the Bitterroot Mountains, stopping at Big Hole (August 9). They continued southeast through the Bitterroot Mountains until they got to Camas Creek (August 18). Leaving Camas Creek they headed through Targhee Pass, Yellowstone Park and over the Absarokas Mountains, traveling northeast to Canyon Creek (September 13). By the time they reached Canyon Creek they had lost most of their strong men and were left with mostly elders, women and children. They headed north with hopes of reaching Canada and safety. Up until this time the Nez Percé had successfully fought eighteen battles. They had reached Cow Island on September 25th and five days later fought their last battle just forty miles (64.40 km) from Canada.

Over what kind of land did they travel—deserts, valleys, mountains and rivers?

It took them 108 days to travel this route. How long would it take you today to travel this same route using modern transportation?

Study a Leader

There is much more you can learn about these leaders you have just read about. There are many more leaders that can be studied. Do some research on one of the leaders and write a report on what you found out about his life. Here is a list you may want to choose from.

Other Noted Leaders of the 19th Century

Juan Antonio (Cahuilla Kawia), 1783-1863
Arapoosh (River Crow), 1790-1834

Big Bow (Kiowa), 1830-1900
Big Foot (Miniconjou Sioux), 1825-1890
Black Hawk (Sauk), 1767-1838
Blacksnake (Seneca), 1760-1859

Cochise (Chiricahua Apache), 1812-1874

Dennis Wolf Bushyhead (Cherokee), 1826-1898
Dohosan (Kiowa), 1805-1866

Eskaminzim (Coyotero Apache), 1825-1870

Flatmouth (Chippewa), 1774-1860
Stephen Foreman (Cherokee), 1807-1881

Ganado Mucho (Navajo), 1809-1893
Gelelemend (Delaware), 1722-1811
Francis Godfry (Miami), 1790-1840
John Grass (Teton Sioux), 1837-1918

Hollow-Horn Bear (Brule Sioux), 1850-1913

Irateba (Mohave), 1814-1878
Iron Tail (Oglala Sioux), 1850-1916

Little Raven (Arapaho), 1817-1889
Little Wolf (Northern Cheyenne), 1820-1904
Looking Glass (Nez Percé), 1823-1877
Fred Lookout (Osage), 1860-1949

Manuelito (Navajo), 1818-1894

Pete Nocoma (Comanche), 1825-1861

Opothleyaholo (Creek), 1798-1862
Oshkosh (Menominee), 1795-1858

Quanah Parker (Comanche), 1845-1911
John W. Quinney (Mahican), 1797-1855

Schonchin (Modoc), 1815-1873
Seattle (Suquamish/Duwamish), 1788-1866
Sitting Bull (Hunkpapa Sioux), 1834-1890
Spotted Tail (Brule Sioux), 1823-1881
Standing Bear (Ponca), 1829-1908
Stumbling Bear (Kiowa), 1832-1903

Toolhulhulsote (**Nez Percé**), 1810-1877
Two Strike (Sioux), 1832-1915

Sarah Winnemucca (Paviotso Paiute), 1844-1891
Allen Wright (Choctaw), 1825-1885

Researching the Battles

There were many battles fought during this century you may want to research. Study one of these and report your findings. Read several sources to see if the writing is biased and if what happened was fair to the people.

Black Hills

Battle of Big Axe

Battle of Big Hole

Battle of Fallen Timbers

Battle of Horseshoe Bend

Battle of the Hundred Slain

Battle of Lake George

Battle of New Orleans

Battle of Point Pleasant

Battle of the Thames

Battle of Tippecanoe

Sand Creek Massacre

Little Big Horn

Battle of Wounded Knee

Some of these battles were actually fought before the eighteenth century. Which was the battle that ended the wars?

The Artists

During the nineteenth century, Indian art was not well-known to most and was just the beginning of its appreciation. If we look at Native American Indian artifacts, we know that art is certainly a part of the Indian culture.

Datsolalee (Washo), 1835-1925

Datsolalee was one of the most accomplished basket designers and weavers of her generation. Basket weaving was a main source of income for many of the Washo people. Datsolalee was well-known for her craft and respected among her people. It was said that Datsolalee would first see her baskets in dreams before she made them. Her work was so intricate that she often had weavings that would take her a year to make. In 1930, five years after her death, one of her baskets sold for $10,000, which was a lot of money in those days, especially for a basket. In her lifetime she may have produced almost 300 woven objects, maybe more. The baskets were made of cured fern fibers and willow reed in their natural colors. Her works can be found all over the world in museums and in private collections.

GA1322

Atsidi Sani
(Navajo)
1830-1870

Atsidi Sani was the first to introduce silversmith art to the Navajo people. He learned his craft from a Mexican ironsmith called Nakai Tsosi. Sani started out by making bridle ornaments and then other objects using silver coins. When other Navajos showed interest in this skill, he taught them.

Sani developed a deep pride and artistic skill in this silversmithing craft, and it showed in his work. This was the beginning of what has become a main source of income for many Navajo families today.

Crescencio Martinez (San Ildefonso Pueblo), 1890-1918

Crescencio Martinez was one of the very first known Pueblo artists. He started painting pottery and later painted with watercolors. He was commissioned to paint a series of ceremonial dances for the Museum of New Mexico and the School of American Research in Santa Fe. His work was exhibited in New York with the Society of Independent Artists.

Sadly, he died of pneumonia in 1918, before he was able to complete the ceremonial dance series, and also before his art was shown at the American Museum of Natural History in New York in 1920. Crescencio Martinez's paintings became well-known, especially among the Europeans because they were not aware that any "Indian paintings" existed.

GA1322

The Florida Boys

James Bear's Heart	Howling Wolf	William Cohoe	Zotom
(Cheyenne)	(Cheyenne)	(Cheyenne)	(Kiowa)
1851-1882	1850-1924	1854-1924	1853-1913

In December of 1874 seventy-two Plains Indians were taken to prison at Fort Marion near St. Augustine, Florida. Four of these men developed their artistic skills while they were in prison. Art materials were provided. The sketchbooks and drawings created by these four men are now treasured Native American Indian art.

James Bear's Heart sketched pictures, as did the others. They also used Indian symbolism and traditional Indian artistic expression. William Cohoe painted pictures of his memories. Howling Wolf completed twelve pictures of Cheyenne life as he remembered, from the coming of the first white man to the death of Roman Nose. Most of their lives as artists were short, except for Zotom, who later found his artistic skills to be a financial advantage. While he was in prison Zotom painted. His paintings on fans became quite popular. In 1898 he painted model tipi coverings for the Omaha Exposition. Included in his work was a series of buckskin shield covers.

Nampeyo
(Hopi)
1859-1942

Nampeyo was born in 1859. She learned the art of ceramics by watching her grandmother make ceramic pots. She used her creative talent to revitalize the old art of ancient pots. Her artistic style was so different from the other Hopi potters, and her beautifully designed pots became very popular. There was a trading company in the Grand Canyon area by the name of the Fred Harvey Company that employed Nampeyo and helped to make her artwork known worldwide. On July 20, 1942, Nampeyo died and her daughter Fannie, who had learned the art from her mother was able to continue the traditional ceramic artwork of her mother.

Other Artists of the Time
Angel DeCora Dietz (Winnebago), 1871-1919, artist/illustrator
Charles Edensaw (Haida), 1839-1924, carver
Ramona (Chuilla), 1865-1922, basket weaver
Hosteen Klah (Navajo), 1867-1937, weaver/sand painter

Activities

Research an Artist
You may find it interesting to research some of the other artists mentioned, or even to find out about the other forms of art.

For example: What can you find out about sand painting? Who does sand painting and in what cultures can sand paintings be found?

Basket Weaving
Invite a local basket weaver to demonstrate the weaving of baskets for the class. Maybe this artist can bring samples of the many different kinds of weavings that are done.

Make a display on a bulletin board of the different types of baskets you can find locally; pictures can be used if real baskets are not available.

Visit a local museum where Indian baskets are displayed. It could be a fun field trip and very interesting as well.

Using a variety of weaving materials, you could weave a basket of your own. You can find basket weaving books in a library that will show you some different styles you can choose from.

GA1322

Pottery

Materials:
modeling clay or red earth clay
water
art utensils
poster paints

Taking a large clump of clay, use your hands to form a pot or bowl to your liking. Smooth out any rough spots with your hands and wet down with water. (If your school has a potter's wheel, this could be used if you have someone to demonstrate it.) Try not to leave any bubbles in the clay so that the bowl does not crack when it is fired. When the pot or bowl is the exact shape you desire, you may want to make designs in the clay using the utensils for carving. When this is done, bake the object in a kiln or oven. After it is baked or fired, you can paint designs on the pot.

Silversmith Speaker and Demonstration

Find a local silversmith and invite this person to speak to the class and demonstrate how silver jewelry is made. Ask about the different methods and how Indian silver work may be different or similar from what this artist does.

Display silver Native American Indian jewelry. Pictures can be used if there is no jewelry available.

Field Trips

There may be local museums or retail stores that sell Native American Indian jewelry, arts and crafts. Be sure to ask if the store carries only authentic articles. If not, ask the manager to show you the jewelry that is authentic. Some items displayed or sold in stores and museums are quite expensive. It is important to view what is displayed with care.

GA1322

Authors and Others

Inshtamaze, the last of the Omaha chiefs, was also known as Joseph La Flesche. He was the son of a French trader and an Osage woman. He married twice and had several children who became quite successful in life. Of the La Flesche children Susette, Susan and Francis were best known.

Joseph La Flesche felt that it was important for his children to have knowledge and respect for their Indian traditions and also to be educated and raised in the way of the Whites.

The Children of Joseph La Flesche

Susan La Flesche
(Omaha/Osage)
1865-1915

Susan La Flesche in 1889 became the first female Native American Indian doctor of medicine. As a government doctor she would treat the people on the reservation traveling from place to place on horseback. It is said that before her own death she had doctored nearly every Omaha tribal member on the reservation.

Francis La Flesche
Zhogaxe
(Omaha/Osage)
1857-1932

As a boy, Francis La Flesche participated in traditional dances and ceremonies and experienced some of the last buffalo hunts on the Plains. When he was a young man of twenty-four, he worked with Alice Fletcher, a well-known anthropologist of the time. He assisted her with interpretation and research. Together they produced a thorough study of the Omaha tribe. He worked with the U.S. Senate Committee on Indian Affairs in Washington, D.C. Law was the major focus of his education, and he was very concerned and interested in his people. During his life he wrote a book about his experiences as an Indian student in a white school, *The Middle Five: Indian Boys at School*. Among his accomplishments is a complete study of the rites and rituals of the Osage tribe, the *Osage Dictionary* and together with Alice Fletcher published *A Study of Omaha Music*. He also influenced Charles Wakefield Cadman's composition of "From the Land of Sky Blue Waters."

Susette La Flesche
Inshtatheumba
(Omaha/Osage)
1854-1903

After completing her education at Elizabeth Institution for Young Ladies in New Jersey, Susette La Flesche returned to teach at the reservation school. She too had great interest in her people and the just affairs of all Indians, especially the Poncas. She became a well-known speaker and toured the United States and England to speak about Indian rights. Susette followed the belief of her father and also felt that education and assimilation were important for Indian people but that it was also most important to keep the traditional practices and cultural values alive.

Carlos Montezuma
Wassaja
(Yavapai)
1867-1923

At the age of five, Wassaja was captured by some Pima Indians. His mother tried to find him but was killed in the process. Later in Florence, Arizona, he was sold by these Indians to an Italian man who was a photographer and a prospector; his name was Carlos Gentile. This man took Wassaja away from the Southeast to Chicago. Wassaja was baptized Carlos Montezuma. He completed his education and became a doctor of medicine.

Throughout his career he strongly supported the rights of Indians. He often criticized the Bureau of Indian Affairs and wanted it gone. He clearly did not like the reservation system. Carlos Montezuma became so well-known that he was twice offered positions with the BIA, which included a job as the director. He did not want the positions and did not want to accept the offers. When the Blacks were given citizenship, he was angry that the Indian people were still considered aliens.

Early in the twentieth century he started a magazine that wrote about Indian affairs, and from the writing of this came some very important words that have often been used, "Let My People Go."

Other 19th Century Portraits

Elias Boudinot (Cherokee), 1803-1839, author
Amos Bad Heart Bull (Oglala Sioux), 1869-1913, artist/historian

Jesse Chisholm (Cherokee), 1805-1868, guide/trader
George Copway (Ojibwa), 1818-1863, first Native American author
Curly (Crow), 1859-1923, scout

John N.B. Hewitt (part Tuscarora), 1859-1937, anthropologist
George Hunt (Kwakiutl), 1854-1933, ethnologist/tribal informant

Ishi (Yahi), 1860-1916, museum orator/last of Stone Age people in North America

Peter Jones (Ojibwa), 1802-1856, author
William Jones (Fox), 1871-1909, Indian ethnologist/author

Simonb Pokagen (Potawatomi), 1830-1899, chief/author
Alexander Lawrence Posey (Creek), author/educator

Sacajawea (Shoshoni), 1784-1812, interpreter

Two Guns White Calf (Pikuni Blackfoot), 1872-1934

Nancy Ward (Cherokee), 1738-1824, influenced tribe
Whilliam Whipple Warrne (Chippewa), 1825-1853, author
Winema (Modoc), 1848-1932, influenced tribe

Chauncey Yellow Robe (Yanktonai Sioux), 1870-1930, educator

Activity

Portrait Report

Select one of the people mentioned in this chapter and write or tell all that you found to the class.

A tribe you may not have heard of before is the Yahi. They were a part of the Yana people, living in the northern California area near Mount Lassen. They were a tribe that became victims of the famous Gold Rush of 1849. Many settlers began moving west to California during that time, seeking their fortune. These intruders threatened the lives of the Native people that were living on the land at the time.

The Yahi people could not protect themselves. They would find places to hide during the day so that they would not be found and then go out in the dark of night to look for food. After nearly twenty years of living in fear and being killed little by little, the Yahi people were slowly destroyed and became few in number. By 1911 there was only one person left of the Yahi tribe.

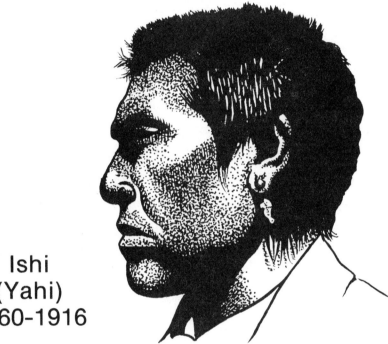

Ishi
(Yahi)
1860-1916

That one survivor of the Yahi tribe was Ishi, often referred to as the last of the Stone Age people in North America. He spent much of his life running, living in fear and trying to survive. It was in 1911 that Ishi was found alone, starving and scared. The people who found him in Oroville contacted Dr. Alfred L. Kroeber from the Museum of Anthropology at Berkeley. The doctor took Ishi back to the museum, gave him a job at the museum and took care of him. He was responsible for naming him Ishi, which means "man" in the Yahi language.

There happened to be a man at the museum who knew Ishi's language and was able to communicate with him. It was during his stay at the museum that Ishi shared information about his people, their customs, their religious rituals and beliefs. For the last four and a half years of his life, Ishi lived on the museum grounds and worked hard to make sure that the history of his people be preserved in the museum through the information he shared.

Even with all that he had experienced in his lifetime, he was a friendly and well-loved man. He contracted tuberculosis and died in 1916. The information he shared of his people was written and is preserved in the Museum of Anthropology at Berkeley.

GA1322

Activities

Fill In

1. Chief Joseph was a member of the _____ tribe and led his people over four states trying to get them to _____ .

2. Chief Joseph spent much of his life trying to get the government to return his people to

_____ .

3. Red Cloud was one of the many chiefs who fought for his _____ and his _____ . The trail he was protecting was the _____ .

4. _____ was the first to introduce the skills of silversmithing to the people of the _____ tribe.

5. Crescencio Martinez, a well-known artist of the Southwest, painted on _____ .

6. The Florida Boys, who were Plains Indians imprisoned at Fort _____ , became well-known artists. They were _____ , _____ ,

_____ and _____ .

7. The well-known children of Joseph La Flesche include his daughter _____ who became a doctor, his son _____ who experienced one of the last buffalo hunts, and his daughter _____ who became a well-known speaker in the United States and England.

GA1322

Part Three: Portraits of the Twentieth Century

The Leaders

With the turn of the twentieth century came the ending of many of the old tribal chiefs who had fought for their people and their land. Now they are an important part of the history of the Native American Indian tribes.

Listed here are a few of those chiefs or leaders.

Big Tree (Kiowa), Crazy Snake or Chitto Harjo (Creek), Geronimo (Chiricahua Apache), John Grass (Teton Sioux), Hollow Horn Bear (Brule Sioux), Howling Wolf (Cheyenne), Hump or Etokeah (Miniconjou Sioux), Ignacio (Wiminuche Ute), Iron Tail or Sinte Maza (Oglala Sioux), Chief Joseph (Nez Percé), Little Wolf (Northern Cheyenne), Mountain Chief or Ninastoko (Blackfoot), Naiche (Chiricahua Apache), Quanah Parker (Comanche), Pleasant Porter or Talof Harjo (Creek), Rain in the Face or Iromagaja (Hunkpapa Sioux), Red Cloud (Oglala Sioux), Standing Bear (Ponca), Tendoy (Lemhi Bannock), Two Moon or Ishiéyo (Cheyenne), Wooden Lance or Apiatan (Kiowa) and Young Bear (Fox)

The events of the past brought a cloud of sadness over the once proud and powerful people. They found themselves being told what they needed to do by the strangers who had invaded their land and homes. They were told where they had to live and that their traditional ways and beliefs were wrong. The intruders wanted to change who, what and how they were.

Although treaties were written to look as if agreements were made, for the Native American Indian there was no freedom of choice. What took place was a forced change of many broken promises.

GA1322

Living on reservation lands, the Native American Indian people had the challenge of having to deal with survival and trying to adapt to a different way of life. Generations have come and gone and the populations of the Native Indian people have continued to grow. With the changes came new leaders, new tribal governments, a stronger pride and a growing power of the people. The despair of the past and the present with a need to survive has strongly influenced the movement toward self-sufficiency and the reviving of the old traditions that are so valuable.

New beginnings are not always easy, and the new leaders and the people were faced with much to be accomplished.

In 1967, Chief Dan George, a Salish Chief and honorary Chief of the Suquamish people, spoke in Vancouver at the Canadian Centennial. In his speech he spoke of the sadness and strife of his people and further stated. . .

"Oh, Canada, how can I celebrate with you this Centenary, this hundred years? Shall I thank you for the reserves that are left to me of my beautiful forests? For the canned fish of my rivers? For the loss of my pride and authority, even among my own people? For the lack of my will to fight back? No! I must forget what is past and gone.

"Oh, God in Heaven, give me back the courage of the olden Chiefs. Let me wrestle with my surroundings. Let me again, as in the days of old, dominate my environment. Let me humbly accept this new culture and through it rise up and go on.

"Oh, God! Like the Thunderbird of old I shall rise again out of the sea; I shall grab the instruments of the white man's success—his education, his skills, and with these new tools I shall build my race into the proudest segment of your society. Before I follow the great Chiefs who have gone before us, oh, Canada, I shall see these things come to pass.

"I shall see our young braves and our chiefs sitting in the houses of law and government, ruling and being ruled by the knowledge and freedom of our great land. So shall we shatter the barriers of our isolation. So shall the next hundred years be the greatest in the proud history of our tribes and nations."

At the turn of the century, while speaking to a group of government leaders in Washington, D.C., on January 14, 1879, Chief Joseph was found still fighting for his people. This time, only using his words, he requested that his people be returned to their old home in the Northwest. In his speech are words that speak of the despair.

"I am tired of talk that comes to nothing. It makes my heart sick when I remember all the good words and all the broken promises. There has been too much talking by men who had no right to talk. Too many misinterpretations have been made; too many misunderstandings have come up between the white man about the Indians.

"I have asked some of the Great White Chiefs where they get their authority to say to the Indian that he will stay in one place, while he sees white men going where they please. They cannot tell me.

"I only ask of the government to be treated as all other men are treated. If I cannot go to my own home, let me have a home in a country where my people will not die so fast. . . .

"We only ask an even chance to live as other men live. We ask to be recognized as men. . . ."

Although Chief Joseph was never allowed to return to his home, four years after this speech a group of women and children were allowed to return to their old home in the Northwest.

So with the beginning of the twentieth century came a new birth of an old people. The words of the past echo in the hearts of those who still survive. The Native people now strive for their future.

GA1322

Henry Chee Dodge
Aditsaii
(Navajo)
1860-1947

Through the process of his life, Chee Dodge was left an orphan when his mother, Bisnayanchi, died. He lived with other family members until he was adopted by a family he had met during The Long Walk. When he was eight he was adopted by his aunt's husband, Perry H. Williams. There has been some question regarding his real father's identity. There is some evidence showing that his real father may have been Henry C. Dodge, a white man who was a Navajo agent living in the area at the time of his birth.

Chee Dodge spoke Navajo and was also fluent in English and Spanish. Because of this, his education and his experience, Chee Dodge was capable of being the official interpreter for the Navajo people. In 1884 he was later appointed Tribal Chief by Dennis Riordan, the Superintendent of Indian Affairs, replacing the well-known Head Chief, Manuelito.

In 1923, Henry Chee Dodge was named the first chairman of the newly formed Navajo Tribal Council and held this position for five years. The council was created to represent the tribe and protect its interest with the United States government and other corporations wanting to use the land and the people for their own financial gain.

He met many challenges as the chairman dealing with the U.S. government, oil leases and also dealing with the division of the people. Chee Dodge was later elected to two more terms as Chairman of the Navajo Tribe. Between his first and second terms he continued his involvement in the issues of the people and the tribal government. At the age of 87, well-respected and admired, he died of pneumonia before he could begin his third term in 1947.

Charles Curtis
(Kansa or Kaw)
1860-1936

Charles Curtis was born in 1860 in North Topeka, Kansas. His parents were Orren A. Curtis and Helen Pappan, who was part Kaw. His grandmothers influenced his life greatly. When he was three years old his mother died and his father sent him to live with his grandmother, Permelia Hubbard Curtis, who was a strong Methodist and a very strong Republican. Three years later his grandmother Curtis sent him to live with his maternal grandmother, Julia Pappan, on the Kaw Reservation. As a youngster, he attended an Indian mission school. There he stayed until 1868, when he returned to Topeka. Back with his Grandmother Curtis, she made sure he went to school and taught him the virtues of religion and the importance of the support of the Republican party. It was her understanding of politics that helped to fashion him into the politician that he was.

In 1880 he became a Kansas lawyer. Elected a congressman in 1882, he served in the House of Representatives for eight terms. In 1906 he held a seat in the Senate until his next advancement in the political arena. Then in 1928 he ran for vice president on the Republican ticket with Herbert Hoover as President. Charles Curtis became the first man of Indian blood to be elected to the second highest office in the United States government. He was a controversial leader, and his years as a politician were filled with many achievements and many that were related to Indian issues.

GA1322

Tawaquaptewa
(Hopi)
1882-1960

Tawaquaptewa was born in Oraibi, Arizona, also known as Third Mesa. After his uncle Lololoma died, he was chosen by the clan elders to be chief of their village in 1902. This was not an easy task, and he tried the best he could to lead his people well. The Hopi people were beginning to experience more and more outsiders coming around their villages. Some of the people felt uneasy with this and saw it as an intrusion upon their way of life. They were very open when talking about this dislike of the intrusions. Tawaquaptewa, in his early twenties, knew little of his leadership role and tried to continue on as his uncle had in accepting the white people who were surveying and exploring their land.

There was unrest among the people. They were not thrilled with the behavior of this young leader, and the village people became divided. In order to find a solution to this bitterness, the opposing sides had a tug-of-war game, which was an interesting way to solve the situation without physical injuries. The losers of this game had to leave the village and live somewhere else. Those who disagreed with the friendliness to the Whites were the ones to leave. They moved out of the village and formed the area called Hotevilla.

It was in 1906, shortly after winning the tug-of-war game, that Tawaquaptewa was taken away by Indian Agent Leupp. This young leader was taken to California to be educated at the Riverside Indian School. Although he protested this move, he stayed in California for four years. During his absence there were attempts by Lomahongyoma to overthrow the leadership role of Tawaquaptewa.

When Tawaquaptewa returned he was very angry about what had taken place in his absence and also angry with being taken away from his people. This anger affected his leadership style and also the people of his village. Eventually the people moved away from Third Mesa leaving Tawaquaptewa with only 350 people in the village, which slowly became less and less.

Although he died a lonely old man in 1960, he was well-known for his carvings of Kachina dolls. His style was unique and different from others who carved these ritual dolls.

Activities

Other Leaders You May Want to Study

Laura Miriam Cornelius (Oneida), 1880-1949

Ned Hatathli (Navajo), 1923-1972

Arthur Parker (Seneca), 1881-1955

Popovi Da (San Ildefonso Pueblo), 1923-1971

Do Some Research

Find out what happened to the animals on the Navajo nation because of grange management initiated by John Collier in 1936.

You may also want to find out about The Long Walk and/or the Trail of Tears which were events that took place in history and greatly affected the lives of some of the Native American Indian tribes.

Who were those tribal people and what actually happened?

Tug-of-War Games

These types of games have been around a long time. Here are a few that you might want to try.

Sit Pole Pull

Materials: a smooth pole about 1½″ (3.79 cm) in diameter and 8 to 10 feet (2.4 to 3 m) long

This game is best played on ground that is smooth so that players cannot brace their feet.

With six to twelve players divided equally to make two teams, the players sit on the ground positioning themselves next to the pole that is lying on the ground. They sit as close to each other as possible (sitting just inside of each other's legs) on either side of the pole at opposite ends of each other. Grabbing the pole with the right hand and at waist level, the teams, on the word *go*, start pulling the pole and trying to pull the other team toward themselves.

Other Variations

Pulling with left hands only

Pulling with both hands

GA1322

Another "Pole Pull"

This tug-of-war game is done individually. There are two players, a nine-foot (2.7 m) pole and a strip of colored material or buckskin which is tied directly in the center of the pole and hanging down. Each player holds the end of the pole with both hands. A line is marked on the ground at the feet of the players holding the pole, about seven feet (2.1 m) between. Then another line is drawn directly in the center between the two. Upon hearing the word *pull*, each player tries to pull the other toward himself hand over hand and at waist level. Each player must work hard at staying behind his own line and be careful not to twist the pole. The first to pull the other over the center line calls "coup." You may want to play for two out of three before calling coup.

Kachina Dolls

Tawaquaptewa, even though a sad and angry man, must have found some peace while he made his kachina dolls.

Kachina dolls are symbols that represent the different Hopi gods and the masked dancers who impersonate the super beings. The kachinas are part of the ceremonies of the Pueblo people, especially the Hopi and Zuni Pueblos. Although kachina gods have been around a long time, the dolls have only been made for about one hundred years.

In the Hopi tradition, the dancers of the ceremonies give the dolls to the children of the village as gifts. The dolls themselves are not prayed to but are basically used to teach children the names and the characteristics of the different kachinas. The Hopi have 250 kachinas, representing different aspects of their religion and culture.

The dolls are made from the root of the cottonwood tree. The tools used to carve these dolls are a knife, a metal file and sandstone for smoothing. When the figure is ready, a coat of white clay is painted on the doll before being painted with the colored paint. The older dolls were painted with natural paints made from the earth, and the newer dolls are painted with paints that are bought in stores.

GA1322

Carving Activity

Materials:

Ivory soap bars or balsa wood pieces
dull paring knives or butter knives

You may want to try carving wood or soap bars into dolls of your own. Soap bars carved with butter knives are probably safer for first-time carvers. Instead of dolls, you might want to try carving animals out of your bars of soap. If wood is used, try a soft wood.

If you have chosen to carve with wood, then you also might want to paint your carving with poster paints.

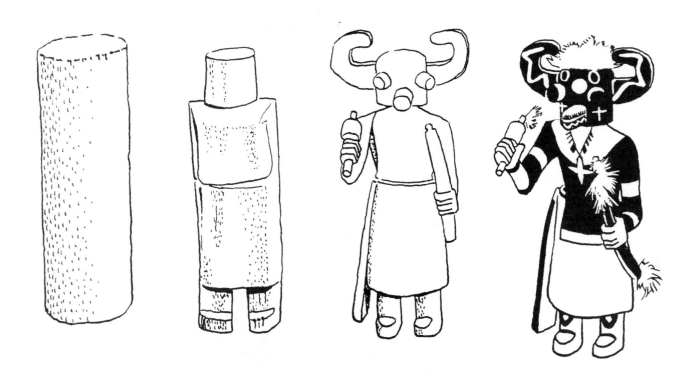

Authors and Others

There are many other personalities of the twentieth century that became well-known. These people range from those who are authors, athletes, anthropologists, doctors, speakers and others. They all reached their own personal fame through hard work.

Ella Carla Deloria
(Anpetu Wastewin)
Yankton Sioux
1888-1971

Ella Deloria was born in July 1888, in the town of Wakpala, South Dakota. She was raised in a religious home, her father being an Episcopalian minister. Her mother, Tipi Sapa, was a Yankton Sioux. Education was an important process of that home and after attending primary and secondary schools, she attended Oberlin College. It was at Columbia University that she received a bachelor of science degree.

In the years that followed she became very interested in the preservation of her native language and culture. In 1929 she worked with Dr. Franz Boas. Together they studied the Siouan language. She became an expert in the cultural history of the Sioux. *Dakota Texts*, published in 1932, was her first book. For many years she wrote about the Dakota culture and the language and lectured throughout the country.

At the age of eighty-three she died of pneumonia and left behind a memory of a woman devoted to her people and their language. Today her written studies on the Sioux language and cultural history are kept at the University of South Dakota and are named in reference as the Ella C. Deloria Project.

GA1322

Charles Alexander Eastman
Ohiyesa
(Santee Sioux)
1858-1939

This man's name may not be familiar to you, but he was very involved in the forming of the Boy Scouts and Camp Fire Girls of America. He established thirty-two Indian YMCA groups throughout the United States when he was a secretary for the Young Men's Christian Association.

Mary Eastman gave birth to Charles Eastman in 1858 in Redwood Falls, Minnesota. When he was young, his father, Jacob Eastman, encouraged him to get an education. During the process of his education, he received a bachelor's degree and was one of the first Indian students to receive a Doctorate of Medicine degree from Boston University.

Eastman was a physician and an author, dedicated to the Sioux people and interested in children. He wrote nine books. *Indian Boyhood* and *The Soul of the Indian* are two of those books. His writing and lecturing helped the general public understand the plight of the Sioux people.

Appointed by President Theodore Roosevelt, he worked with the U.S. government in revising land allotments of the Sioux people in 1903 and later in 1920 as the United States Indian Inspector, verifying the burial place of Sacajawea. When he was seventy-five years old, he received the first Indian Achievement Award. In June of 1939 he died leaving behind many accomplishments of his eighty years of life.

GA1322

A personality of the first half of the twentieth century was a man whose name was known in almost every household. That was Will Rogers.

Will Rogers
(Cherokee)
1879-1935

William Penn Adair Rogers was born on November 4, 1879. It was in 1902 when Will Rogers began his career of performing. After traveling to Argentina, he joined a Wild West Show where he performed rope riding tricks as the Cherokee Kid, using skills he learned on his father's ranch. A few years later he became a vaudevillian, and his success grew as he developed his art of humor. He appeared in musicals on Broadway and in London. From 1914 to 1924 he joined Ziegfeld's Follies and acted in movies. He starred in seventeen movies, acting in roles that were basically his own personality. A charitable man, he donated his money and his time for benefits and charitable organizations during the Depression.

As a writer, Rogers began a weekly newspaper column in 1922. His style and humor became so well loved that he started to write the column every day. He became known as the Cowboy Philosopher. His writing often included humorous remarks about government officials. He also wrote books. Two of the books are *Rogerisms, the Illiterate Digest* and *Letters of a Self-Made Diplomat to His President*.

It was on August 15, 1935, that many people of the nation were saddened when they heard of his death in an airplane that crashed while on its way to the Orient. He was only fifty-six years old when he died. His generosity and his ability to make people laugh were the gifts he shared with many.

GA1322

Along with Will Rogers there are others who chose the area of entertainment for their careers and employment. The very first Native American Indian in films was a Sioux by the name of William Eagleshirt. Others who also pursued careers in acting include Frank Hill, Apache; Jay Silverheels, Iroquois; and Iron Eyes Cody, Cree.

Among the first is Iron Eyes Cody, a Cree, who was born in 1916. He has acted in films for many years, and his latest film was *Ernest Goes to Camp*. Among his biggest concerns are children and elderly people. He spends much of his time at fund-raisers which help benefit people on the reservations. The Hope Ranch in Montana and the Don Drowty Youth Foundation are just a few of those organizations. Iron Eyes Cody also travels to many reservation areas speaking to the people about the importance of staying away from alcohol and the unity of all tribal people.

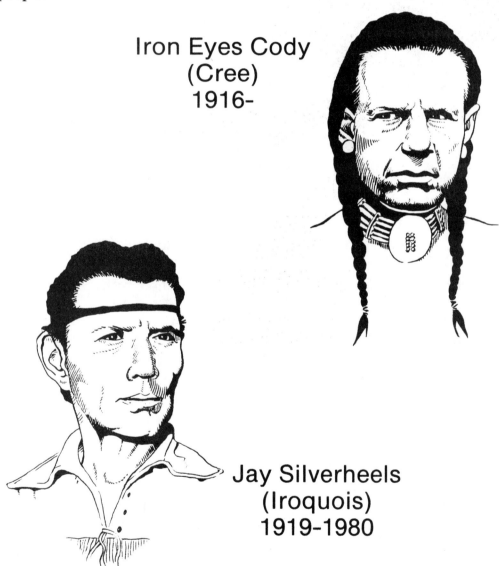

Iron Eyes Cody
(Cree)
1916-

Jay Silverheels
(Iroquois)
1919-1980

Jay Silverheels, an Iroquois, was another actor who was best known for his role as Tonto in *The Lone Ranger*. He initially was a boxer and ice skater but had lost the use of one eye. During his later years he was living in the Motion Picture Home for actors. Before his death in 1980, he was recognized and honored on the Sidewalk Hall of Fame in Hollywood.

GA1322

Anthony Numkena
(Karok-Hopi)
1942-

As a young boy of seven, Anthony Numkena began his career as a child actor. He attended the Sherman Institute, which is now an Indian school. Many southern California Indians were involved in the making of films. A television star by the name of Tim McCoy had a Saturday program where he presented information about Indians. He wanted authentic Native American Indians on his program, and it was on this show that Anthony Numkena began acting.

During the late Forties and early Fifties, child actors had to have work permits to work in the movies and were required to attend school. His teacher at the time was Mrs. Clampton, and one of his classmates was Shirley Temple. He also attended school with the Disney Mouseketeers.

In 1952 he played the main child character in *Pony Soldier*, with Tyrone Power, produced by 20th Century Fox. *Destination Gobie* was another film where his role was a Mongolian child. Other performances, including several Disney productions, were *Westward Ho the Wagons* and *Brave Eagle*. He also appeared on television in *The Loretta Young Show, Wagon Train* and *The Mickey Mouse Club*.

When asked how he felt about portraying other tribal groups or portraying the Mongolian child, he simply stated that acting was a job and he enjoyed his work. Today he works as an X-ray technician and does think about acting again.

Activities

Other Authors of the Time

William Thomas Gilcrease (Creek), 1890-1962
Gertrude Simmons Bonnin (Yankton Sioux), 1875-1938
Edward Pasqual Dozier (Santa Clara Pueblo), 1858-1939
Rollie Lynn Riggs (Cherokee), 1899-1954

Write a Report

Complete a report on one of the persons mentioned above or one of the actors.

Fill In

Match the following descriptions with these proper names: Will Rogers, Ella Deloria, Jay Silverheels, Charles A. Eastman and William Eagleshirt.

1. _____ was once a boxer who lost the use of one eye and went on to become a well-known television star who was honored on the Sidewalk Hall of Fame in Hollywood.

2. The first Native American Indian actor in the movie industry was _____ .

3. One of the founders of the Boy Scouts and Camp Fire Girls of America was _____ .

4. Books and studies written about the Sioux language and the cultural history were authored by _____ .

5. _____ was a humorist and writer.

The Athletes

In the world of sports there are several athletes who have made their own great personal achievements and are truly an asset to the Native American Indian populations.

James Francis Thorpe
(Sac/Fox)
1888-1953

At the 1912 Olympic Games in Sweden, Jim Thorpe won gold medals in both the decathalon and pentathlon. King Gustav of Sweden described him as "The Greatest Athlete in the World." A year after he had won his medals, it was found that Jim Thorpe had played baseball and was paid money, a mere $25. Because of this, the Amateur Athletic Union decided that his amateur status should be removed, and he was forced to return his Olympic medals and his achievements were removed from the Olympic records.

Although saddened by the turn of events, Jim Thorpe continued his athletic career. From 1913-1919 he played professional baseball for the New York Giants, the Cincinnati Reds and the Boston Braves. Later he also became well-known as a great professional football player and was the first president of the American Professional Football Association in 1920. In 1950 he was voted as the best athlete of the first half of the twentieth century by the Associated Press. Among his honors he was also named to both the college and professional football halls of fame.

For a man who also excelled in archery, swimming, hockey, basketball and other forms of sports, Jim Thorpe's athletic career slowly declined, and the strong and powerful athlete was found working in movies as a stunt man and at other odd jobs. It was said that he never got over his medals being taken from him. Toward the late Forties, his life did begin to improve, but in 1953 he died of a heart attack.

GA1322

In 1955 the National Football League established the Jim Thorpe Memorial Trophy for the most valuable player award. It was not until 1973, twenty years after his death, that the Amateur Athletic Union finally replaced his records in the Olympic records. Although his status was finally recognized, his medals were still being withheld from his family. His three daughters worked hard to restore their father's honors and clear his name. Finally, in 1984 the medals he had won were returned and given to his daughter Charlotte. There are many people today who regard Jim Thorpe as a great athletic legend.

Native American Indians in Baseball

There were many Native American Indians in the sport of baseball. Even though, from 1884 to 1947 there was a time of much segregation in the sports world, the Native American Indians who were playing in the league were the most visible, unlike their African American peers. These men who played baseball, even in their height of popularity, were often referred to as "Chiefs," a common nickname for all those players who were of Indian blood. These encounters were just a subtle indication of the discrimination they may have encountered. For most of these Indian athletes, this nickname was not appreciated nor is it welcome today.

Well-Known Baseball Players of the Time
Chief Meyers (Chauilla)
Allie Reynolds (Creek)
Rudy York (Cherokee)
Louis Le Roy (Seneca)
Ben Tincup (Cherokee)
Moses Yellowhorse (Pawnee)
Elon Hogsett (Cherokee)

GA1322

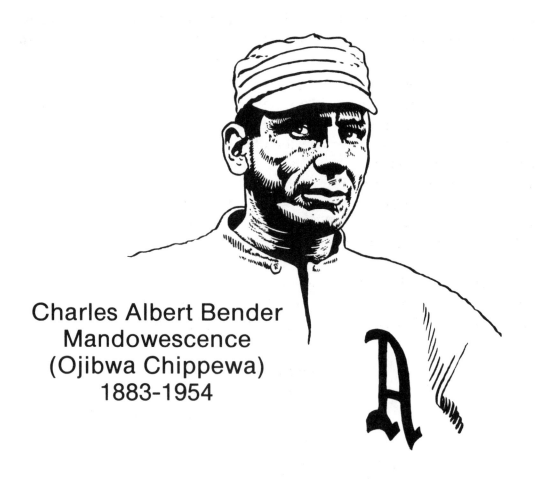

Charles Albert Bender
Mandowescence
(Ojibwa Chippewa)
1883-1954

Seven years before his big success as a fastball pitcher, Charles Albert Bender, at the age of 13, chose to leave the White Earth Reservation and his family in Minnesota. He went to the Carlisle Indian School in Pennsylvania and also experienced the Quaker way of life while on school outings. He received a degree from Dickinson College. It was probably because of his education and the influence of the Quaker people that he did not view professional baseball as an occupation. Personally he did not see his accomplishments as a positive reflection of or to his people. Regardless of how he felt, his life and achievements are certainly a reflection of his personal courage, strength and athletic abilities.

In 1903 he started his baseball career with the Philadelphia Athletics and became the leading pitcher of the team. While he was with the A's they won the American League pennant five times and three World Series. Bender was a noted superstar of the time.

Even though he had other interests in life, Bender continued with baseball as his main career. After his professional career as a ball player, he went on and coached the U.S. Naval Academy team and the Chicago White Sox. In 1939 he returned to the Philadelphia Athletics as a talent scout and later coached. He was elected to the Baseball Hall of Fame in 1953.

GA1322

Although what you have just read deals mostly with athletes in baseball, it is important to note that there are other very talented and well-known Native American Indian athletes. Here are a few.

Johnny Bench (Choctaw), baseball
Patti Lyon Catalano (Mimac), marathon runner
Stephen Francis Cosgrove (Sioux), baseball
John Old Crow (Cherokee), professional football
Bertram Hayman (Modoc), baseball
Martinez Heath (Warm Springs), jockey
Alvaro Lopez (Yaqui), boxer
Wahoo McDaniel (Cherokee), professional wrestler
Billy Mills (Sioux), 1964 Olympics, 10,000 meter winner
Joe Thornton (Cherokee), World's Champion Olympic archer
Louis Tewanima (Hopi), 1912 Olympics, track and field
Carol Allen Weston (Quapaw-Euchee-Cherokee), shotput
Roxie Woods (Athapascan-Eskimo), dogsled runner

Activities

There are many nicknames that people of different racial origins hear themselves called.

Are you aware of any of those names, or have you had personal experience of being called a name because of your ethnic group?

Take time to discuss the difference between a nickname that is acceptable and one that is not.

How does a person feel when being called an unacceptable nickname? Is it ever okay?

Activities

Athlete Hero

Choose one of the athletes mentioned on the previous page and research the life of this person. Write a report about what you learned about this person.

Athlete Find

What is your favorite form of sports? See if you can find a Native American Indian who participates in, or has participated in, your favorite sport. This person can be either an amateur or professional athlete.

Games

Native American Indians, both old and young, have enjoyed and participated in traditional sports and games for years. Many years ago games were played for fun, entertainment and the building of skills. Children played many games that children play today such as games of tag, follow the leader, hide and seek, ring 'round games, skipping rope and string cradle games.

With no stores available to buy toys, many objects needed for games were usually found in the environment, like logs, branches, stones, shells, fruit pits and other basic materials.

As with most games, it takes much practice and participation to build skills, and the physical exercise also helps to build strong athletic bodies.

Here are some games that you may enjoy.

The Twisted Trail Relay (Kiowa Trail)
(Woodland-Northwest Coast)

Played outdoors or indoors in a large room or gym with two equal-numbered teams.

Materials: paper plates or similar markers (6)

Start
‾‾‾‾‾‾

O O

O O

O O

O O

O O

O O

‾‾‾‾‾‾
Finish

The start and finish lines should be marked on the ground or use masking tape indoors. The markers are placed in two rows with four feet (1.22 m) between each marker, beginning ten feet (3.04 m) from the starting line and ending ten feet (3.04 m) from the finish line.

The team players line up in front of the start line. The appointed "caller" starts the relay by shouting "Go!" The first player of each of the teams takes off running. When the runner reaches each marker, he/she circles it and moves on to the next. When the runner reaches the finish line, the next player in line takes off. Each player takes his turn when the last member of the team has completed the twisted trail. The first team to finish is the winner.

To make this relay more challenging, the team runners can be asked to race the trail up and back before touching the next person in line.

The Crab Race
(Northwest Coast)

This race can take place outdoors or indoors. Children of the Northwest Coast were very aware of how crabs run. Find out how a crab does run. This is how you will run your crab race. The distance between the start and finish lines can be about forty feet (12.16 m), or shorter if desired. The players then line up about four feet (1.22 cm) apart. When the caller says, "Go!" the players drop quickly onto hands and knees and race like crabs to the finish line. The first to crab crawl all the way is the winner.

For More of a Challenge

When reaching the finish line, the players crab crawl back to the starting line without turning their bodies around or stopping. The first one back is the winner.

GA1322

The Kick Stick Race
(Zuni)

For the Zuni people, this race can also be a very important ceremonial event with the object of bringing rain. People of all ages participate in this race. It can be played either as individuals or in teams.

To prepare for this race you will need to find a piece of firewood or stick about 5″ (12.7 cm) long and ¾″ (1.9 cm) in diameter. A stick is needed for each player or team of players. You may want to decorate your sticks by painting designs on them. When they are dry you are ready to race.

A straight, round or oval-shaped area, about 100 to 500 yards (91 to 455 m) in length, should be marked off outdoors for the course of the race. You may choose to use your school track grounds for this game.

The race is started by laying the sticks in a straight line about three feet (.91 m) apart. Each player stands behind his/her stick facing in the direction of the run. When the caller or referee shouts "Go!" each player kicks the stick forward toward the direction of the finish line, running to the stick and then kicking it again until the kicker reaches the finish line. You may be disqualified if you touch the stick with your hands. Should a player kick another player's stick, the same thing may be done to his/her stick by another player, depending on the decision of the referee. The first player to reach the finish line is the winner.

When racing in teams, two or three players on each team kick the same stick. Two players on a team are preferred.

Have fun!

GA1322

The Artists

Many Native American Indian artists have become well-known throughout the world by those who have learned to appreciate Native American Indian art forms and styles.

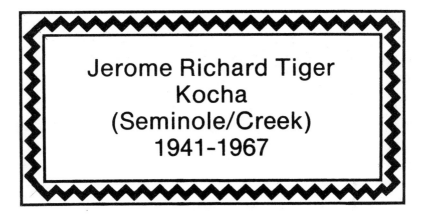

There are many Native American Indian artists who have a deep respect and admiration for Jerome Richard Tiger. His unique style has influenced their own individual artistic styles.

Jerome Tiger was born in Tahlequah, Oklahoma, in July 1941. Before he joined the U.S. Naval Reserve, he studied at the Cleveland Engineering Institute in Ohio. It was in 1962, two years after he completed his naval training, that he seriously began his career in art. He sent some of his art samples to the Philbrook Indian Art Annual.

For five years Jerome Tiger painted scenes of Indian life and traditional mythology. His original paintings became very popular. His traditional style and his individual expression was what artists and art enthusiasts loved. As a young man in his early twenties, he was the most sought after Indian artist of the time. Even today his paintings are displayed in the Museum of the American Indian.

It was in 1967, when he was only twenty-six years old, that his life ended tragically when he was playing with a small gun and it suddenly fired. Although his death took place nearly a quarter of a century ago, Jerome Tiger and his art are still remembered.

GA1322

Pueblo Potters

Julian Martinez
(San Ildefonso Pueblo)
1897-1943

Maria Montoya Martinez
(San Ildefonso Pueblo)
1884-

Together Julian and Maria Martinez became well-known as master potters. They contributed to the process of ceramic art in the Southwest. Julian enjoyed painting and found a new interest while working on an archaeological dig close to their home area. They studied the old designs and shapes by piecing the potsherds together and seeing the historic pots that were found. Later, while working at the State Museum in Santa Fe, New Mexico, they studied the artifacts that were stored in the museum. Maria began to form her pots after those she had studied, while Julian used the designs in painting on their pots. Around 1920 they found a way to produce the ancient technique of black satin finish pottery. This method became their trademark and has won them honors in the world of pottery.

70

GA1322

Basket Weavers

Mary Knight Benson
(Pomo)
1878-1930

William Benson
(Kalanaponen Pomo)
1862-1937

At the turn of the twentieth century, a woman from Pasadena, who was an Indian art dealer, met a Pomo couple living in the north central area of California. They had a great artistic skill of weaving beautiful thread baskets.

Mary and William Benson were actually from different individual tribes, which were part of what is known as the Pomo people. There are about seventy-two different communities who had lived in the Potter Valley. William is of the Kalanaponen tribe, of the eastern area, and Mary is from one of the central area communities.

The decorated Pomo baskets were usually made by women, but a few men did weave. William Benson is one of the better known. Pomo baskets were woven from willow shoots, sedge roots and sometimes thread and feathers.

It was in the Yokayo area that this couple lived and wove their baskets, and where Grace Nicholson first met them in 1905. During a thirty-year period, the Bensons made several baskets that they sent to their friend. Along with the baskets were letters they had written and photographs. These were all saved by Grace Nicholson. This collection is the most detailed in the history of baskets. The collection is now with the National Museum of the American Indian.

Here is a list of other artists. You may want to study more about those already mentioned or choose one of the following:

Awa Tsireh (San Ildefonso Pueblo), 1898-1956
Acree Blue Eagle (Creek), 1909-1959
Fred Beaver (Creek), 1911-
William F. Bigspring (Blackfoot), 1919-
Blackbear Bosin (Comanche/Kiowa), 1921-
Calvin J. Boy (Blackfoot), 1923-
Pop Chalee (Taos Pueblo), 1905-
Goingback Cheltoshey (Cherokee), 1907-
Adele Victor Collins (Chickasaw), 1908-
Oswald White Bear Fredricks (Hopi), 1905-
Carl Nelson Gorman (Navajo), 1907-
Jack Hokeah (Kiowa), 1900-1969
Allan Houser (Chiricahua Apache), 1914-
Mungo Martin (Kwakiutl), 1879-1962
Waldo Mootzka (Hopi), 1910-1940
Stephen Mopope (Kiowa), 1898-1974
Gerald Nailor (Navajo), 1917-1952
Oqwa Pi or Tony Martinez (San Ildefonso Pueblo), 1923-1971
Otis Poledonema (Hopi), 1902-
Ben Quintana (Cochiti Pueblo), 1925-1944
Hart Merriam Schultz (Blackfoot), 1882-1970
Ernest Spybuck (Shawnee), 1883-1949
Quincy Tahoma (Navajo), 1920-1956
Monroe Tsatoke (Kiowa), 1904-1937

Mix and Match

Draw a line from the description on the left to the person on the right that best matches.

Developed the Cherokee Alphabet   Henry Chee Dodge

First Indian Woman Doctor of Medicine   Jim Thorpe

Vice President to Herbert Hoover   Maria Martinez

First Navajo Chairman   Chief Joseph

Winner of Olympic Gold Medals 1912   Charles A. Bender

Famous Pueblo Potter   Charles Curtis

Elected to Baseball Hall of Fame 1953   Susan La Flesche

Great Nez Percé Leader   Sequoya

Did you remember them all?

                    GA1322

Part Four: Portraits of Native American Indians of the Future

The Leaders

The beginning of the twenty-first century brings with it a truth. The Native American Indian can no longer be referred to as the "Vanishing American." With the strong growth of Native American Indian governments and their urgent need for self-sufficiency, there is definitely a future to behold. You will see and hear more and more about the tribal people and their leaders as time passes. The growth of governments and the people will bring about many advancements and achievements.

The Native American Indian populations are growing in numbers and with this comes financial problems for the people and necessary change. The independent tribes and their people will be needing to make some very important decisions for the betterment of all their people. It will be interesting to see the process and to witness the outcome of events yet to take place in the years ahead. It is a challenge which is not easy.

Today there are many individuals who are making a difference, and their efforts are impacting the future of their people. The persons mentioned here are only a few individuals who are meeting that challenge. Through their dedication and capabilities, we will see the effects of their leadership. They, along with their people, are building their future, and their achievements will bring about a better tomorrow.

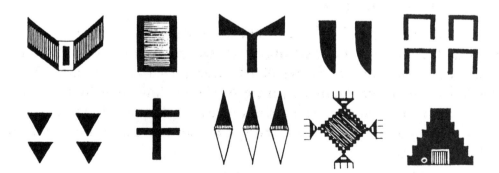

74

Wilma P. Mankiller
(Cherokee)
1945-

In 1987 the people of the Cherokee Nation, which is the second largest Native American Indian tribe in the United States, elected Wilma Mankiller as Principal Chief of the Cherokee Nation. She is the first woman to serve as chief of her tribe.

During the later years of the Fifties, the Mankiller family of eleven children and their parents were forcefully relocated by the BIA (Bureau of Indian Affairs) to the area of San Francisco, California. Leaving their home in Oklahoma was difficult. They had to deal with the change of living in an unfamiliar city, which is very different from life on the reservation. The relocation of the Mankiller family, and other families, was the answer the BIA came up with for what was supposed to be a better way of life.

After graduating from high school, Wilma Mankiller continued her education in sociology and worked as a social worker. She married and had two daughters. In 1969 there was a group of demonstrators who took over the island of Alcatraz for eighteen months. Their mission was to let the public know about the unfair treatment of Native American Indians. Wilma Mankiller became very interested in what the demonstrators were doing, and she helped to raise funds for the American Native Rights and their cause. She became more and more involved in the support of the Indian issues.

Later she divorced her husband and with her children moved back to her grandfather's land on the reservation, where she built a house. By 1977 she was working for the Cherokee Nation as an economic stimulus coordinator. She continued on with her education and received a bachelor's degree from the Flaming Rainbow University. She then worked as a program development specialist. It was in 1981 that she founded the Community Department for the Cherokee Nation, which became very successful.

GA1322

Although she is busy with tribal matters, she finds time to travel around the country speaking about issues concerning the Cherokee Nation and other tribal people. Her message is that all people can learn from the traditional tribal cultures about the oneness of all living things and that human life is very dependent upon the natural world that we are slowly destroying.

As a leader she knows that important decisions should be made only after carefully thinking through the effects of decisions fifty to seventy years in the future. Ms. Mankiller works for and expects the renewal and strengthening of Native people all over North America.

GA1322

Peterson Zah
(Navajo)
1937-

The Navajo tribe is the largest tribe in the United States, with a census population of at least 160,000 members, and it is rapidly growing. The Navajo land covers about 25,000 square miles (64,750 sq. km) and is located within the three states of New Mexico, Arizona and Utah. With a need for unity, leadership and the desire to have control over their social, economical and political independence, the "Dineh" (Navajo people) have once again chosen as their leader Peterson Zah.

Peterson Zah spent his youth in the traditional community of Low Mountain, located in the central part of the main reservation. It is known as the Navajo/Hopi Joint-Use Area in Arizona. As a child he was not aware of anything more than the environment in which he lived. The people of the area practiced the art of dry farming and raising sheep. His father never completed his education, and his mother, who never went to school, sold her weaving to help with the family income. In the Low Mountain area there were few roads and only a couple of families had vehicles. The Zah family would travel to the local trading post, almost twenty-five miles (40.25 km) away. It took them two days to travel by horse and wagon. It was at this trading post that they would buy sugar, flour and coffee and also learn about a place outside of their home area.

Education for most Indians on reservations meant going to boarding school and leaving home at a very young age. When Peterson Zah was nine years old, he was sent to a school that was over one hundred miles (161 km) from home. His determination and desire to get an education was influenced by his aunts and uncles he would see during the summer months when they were home from school. After graduating from the Phoenix Indian School, he continued on to complete an associate of arts degree from Phoenix College and then later earned a bachelor's degree from Arizona State University.

Zah first began his career in the Navajo government in 1967. He was the assistant to the director of the Dinebeiina Nahiilna Be Agaditahe or DNA. This program helped the people with their legal matters. Because of the work he had accomplished while he was with the DNA, Peterson Zah became very popular. With the growth of his popularity came his election as Chairman of the Navajo Tribe in 1983. During this term he dealt with many serious problems that had been around for a long time. The Navajo government and people have experienced many difficulties over the years, and they look to their leader to make things better, a big responsibility for the person elected.

In 1987 the elections changed the hands of leadership. After three years away from office, he was reelected to the very challenging position as tribal president. It was in 1990, the fall session, that the Council Delegates of the Navajo Nation mandated that the title positions of chairman and vice chairman be changed to the titles of president and vice president. The new titles did not bring a change of duties and responsibilities.

President Zah knows the challenges he faces and also that he has a lot of work ahead. This well-respected and charismatic leader spoke to the press just after his election. He was quoted as saying, "The first order of business is going to be putting the tribe back together." With so many things needing to be done, it will take time and also the patience, support and assistance of his people. The unity President Zah speaks of is very important to the success and advancement of the Navajo people and their government.

Activities

The Size of the Navajo Nation
Looking at a map, find out where the boundary lines are for the Navajo Reservation. After you find them, outline the area and see if you can find a state that is about the same size. What is the name of the state?

There are also other areas of Navajo land, better known as the satellite areas of the reservation. They are located in the state of New Mexico. They are the Alamo (Puertocito), Ramah and Canoncito Reservations.

How Far Is Far?
Peterson Zah and his family had to travel about twenty-five miles (40.25 km) to get to the nearest store, and it took them two days. If you had to travel the same distance in a car traveling the posted speed limit of 55 mph, about how long would it take you to reach the store?

As a nine-year-old boy, Zah had to attend a school that was over one hundred miles (1.61 km) from his home. Using a map, see if you can figure out how far a hundred miles (1.61 km) is from where you live. How long would it take you to get there by car?

How would you feel about going to school that far away from home?

Helping Our World
Wilma Mankiller often speaks about the natural world we are fast destroying. What do you think she is talking about? What are we doing that is destroying our natural world? Make a list.

What are some of the things that people are doing today to help with this problem?

What can you as a class do to help in your school and in your homes?

What can you do as an individual to help with the ecology?

Together as a class, plan and follow through with a project to help our Earth and the environment. You might want to get other classes involved in some way.

GA1322

The Artists

In the twentieth century there are many Native American Indian artists who have become recognized by their art. They will certainly continue their popularity on into the twenty-first century. There are probably others who are yet to be discovered.

R.C. Gorman
(Navajo)
1934-

Rudolph Carl Gorman, a Navajo artist, is often referred to as the "Indian Picasso" and is well-known all over the world. He studied at Northern Arizona University and Guam Territorial College. Because of a financial grant he received from the Navajo Tribe, Gorman was able to study art in Mexico City. It was this experience which influenced his artistic style the most. Although he had studied European artists like Rembrandt, Leonardo da Vinci and Michelangelo, R.C. Gorman found his artistic expression of the Mexican artists to be what he could relate to most. He discovered there was a similarity in the Mexican culture to his own Navajo culture. This was when he chose to stop painting like a European artist and when he found true enjoyment painting reflections of his own culture. Over the years, he has used several art mediums, such as watercolors, ceramics and clay, oil pastels, oil paintings, acrylics and silk screens. Living in Taos, New Mexico, R.C. Gorman has a very busy schedule and as a true believer in hard work, his works of art continue to flourish.

GA1322

Other Artists

Here are some other artists you may want to research and report on for your class.

Arnold Aragon (Crow Pueblo), 1953-
James Grayhawk Armagost (Mohican), 1945-
Jean Elaine Meyers Bales (Iowa), 1946-
Parker Boyiddle (Kiowa/Delaware)
T.C. Cannon (Kiowa/Caddo), 1946-
Eula Narcomay Doonkeen (Seminole), 1931-
Brummett Echohawk (Pawnee), 1921-
Robert Lee Freeman (Dakota/Luiseno), 1939-
Benjamin Harjo, Jr. (Seminole/Shawnee)
Douglas Hyde (Nez Percé), 1946-
Barthell Little Chief (Kiowa/Comanche)
Merlin Little Thunder (Southern Cheyenne)
Angelina Median (Acoma/Zia Pueblo)
Jerry Pope (Shawnee), 1941-
Austin Jerald Rave (Minneconjon Sioux), 1946-
Charles H. Red Corn (Osage), 1936-
Bill Rabbit (Cherokee)
Connie Seabourn (Cherokee)
Mark Silversmith (Navajo)
Robert Taylor (Blackfoot Cherokee)
Dana Tiger (Creek/Seminole/Cherokee)
Johnny Tiger, Jr. (Creek/Seminole)
Roger John Tsabetsaye (Zuni), 1941-
Tiller Wesley (Creek)
John Julius Wilnoty (Cherokee), 1940-

GA1322

Others

There are some people who, in some way, affect the lives of others without even being aware they have become heroes in someone else's eyes. Special deeds are not always necessary in the making of heroes. Just making a difference in someone's life is enough.

Many Native American Indian people have heroes. Some are unspoken heroes, some you may have never heard of and maybe never will. For many, the heroes are the people who have endured much and are examples of strength and courage. The people who walked the Trail of Tears, The Long Walk and those who fought the many battles of the past are remembered as heroes. The young and the old, the men and the women, they are all heroes. They have all affected the hearts of those living, and they have made a difference.

A very prominent speaker, looks to the youth he speaks to as heroes. This man, an American Indian educator, trainer and motivator of American Indians, enjoys speaking to the young and helping them to see the power they have within themselves. It is important to him that each individual finds his self-respect and learns that he can rely on the person within to do and be all that is dreamed of and wanted. His name is Howard T. Rainer.

Howard T. Rainer
(Taos Pueblo)

For twenty years Howard Rainer has been presenting workshops and seminars for Native American people. His audiences also include others who wish to hear him speak. His talent for speaking is only part of his personal dream accomplished. He is also a poet, author, photographer, and he has also done some work on motion pictures and television.

GA1322

It is because of his own experiences in life that he has been able to speak so effectively. This man speaks from his heart of the things and people who have most influenced his own life process.

As a child he grew up on the Taos Pueblo Reservation in New Mexico. His grandparents, his father and a special teacher all helped him on his journey. As a young child he felt the hurt of ridicule because of a handicap. He was born with a harelip and cleft palate. As he grew older he was always fearful of others teasing him. It was the special teacher who helped him see the beauty and power within himself. It was this self-discovery that helped him to become the successful man that he is today.

Howard Rainer has affected those he has spoken to in his workshops and presentations. As he continues speaking and conducting workshops, he is helping those who will make a difference for other human beings in the future. What he wants his audience to hear is that it is possible for a person to be whatever it is he or she wants to be and that education is very important in the process of life.

Activities

My Own Heroes

1. When thinking about your own life, do you have a hero or heroes who have made a difference for you? Write about who they are and why and how they have made a difference.

2. Interview an adult. Ask someone in your family if you can interview him/her (for example, an aunt, uncle, father, mother or anyone else). Find out if he/she has a hero that he/she would like to tell you about. Write a report on the interview.

Learning About People with Handicaps

People with handicaps do not want others to feel sorry for them. They just want to be accepted and cared for just like everyone else.

1. Do you know someone who has a handicap?
   What do you know about this person?
   What has this person taught you about life?
   Write about this person.

2. If you do not know someone who has a handicap, talk to others who do, or find someone that does have a handicap and learn all you can about him/her as a person. What did you learn? Write about what you have learned.

   This might be a good time to share what you have written with the group.

3. What are some things that you can do as an individual to help those who are handicapped?

4. Is there a project that you, as a class, can do to help the handicapped people of your community?

My Goals in Life

1. Even though you are young, you can still have goals in life. What are your goals or dreams for yourself? Take time to write about them. You might want to save what you have written so that you can read it when you are older and see if your goals changed.

2. It may also be interesting to interview your parents or grandparents and ask about the goals they had for themselves and if they accomplished those goals. If they did, how did they, and if not, what happened to keep them from doing so? Write a report.

3. Videotape a group of you and your friends in class sharing your goals. This can be viewed at another time.

GA1322

It is important to remember as you study Native American Indians that tribes have different traits, and they should never be considered one and the same. As Betty Baker once said, "I detest authors who portray Indians as one's next door neighbors in costume." Tribes differed as much as Indians and Whites. The tribal beliefs, codes and even the geography of their lands formed thought, action and reaction. Apaches didn't think like Papagos, nor did Hopi react like Iroquois, but few authors take the trouble of slipping inside the Indian's mind. The view is entirely different from the back of the eyes.

There is so much to learn from studying the different tribes. This is only a beginning. There are others yet to read and learn about. While studying this book and doing the activities, you probably have more of an awareness of some of the history of the Native tribal people and hopefully looked at this information "from the back of the eyes."

GA1322

Part Five: Additional Activities

Traditional Foods

When we look at the geographical areas of the North American region, there are five different environments that have influenced the eating habits of those people who lived in those areas, especially when it was a daily practice to live off what the land had to offer.

In the Southwest and the Great Basin areas, which are quite arid, were small animals and some edible plants. Those who lived in the Plains found big game, such as buffalo or bison. East of the Mississippi River there was also big game, small animals and different vegetables that were found in the woodlands. The people living on the West Coast had the sea and the rivers where they found some of their food, like fish and fowl. In the north Arctic area the animals of the land and sea were hunted. In California the major food sources were fruits, acorns, seeds, roots, game animals, fish and fowl.

It is important to note that the Native people took from the land only what they needed for their survival, and when the food sources were low, they would travel on foot to different areas to find food or trade with neighbors.

Today, many Native American Indians enjoy many of the same kinds of foods that you enjoy, such as hamburgers, pizza and others. As in every culture, there are special food dishes that have been traditionally enjoyed and passed on from generation to generation. The Native American Indian people also have special traditional foods that are enjoyed by many.

Activities

Here are a few recipes you might want to try.

Ba Na Ha
    1 pound (720-960 ml) dried peas
    3-4 cups (.45 kg) plain cornmeal
    cornhusks (to soften soak in water)

1. Soak peas in water overnight. Drain. Add water and cook until tender. Drain the liquid into a container. Use this liquid to moisten the cornmeal. Add the peas. You might want to season with salt when cooking the peas.

2. Roll the dough into a ball about two to three inches (5.08 to 7.62 cm) in diameter. Place this in a softened cornhusk, roll and tie securely with strips of cornhusks (much like a tamale).

3. Place the prepared husks in the bottom of a pot with water. Cover and steam for thirty minutes to an hour, or until cooked.

4. This is served as a bread along with stew or cooked meat.

Fry Bread

    4 cups (960 ml) flour
    1 teaspoon (5 ml) salt
    2 tablespoons (30 ml) powdered milk
    1 teaspoon (5 ml) baking powder

    1½ cups (360 ml) warm water
    1 cup (240 ml) lard or shortening

Preparing the Dough

1. In a large bowl sift dry ingredients together. Sifting can be done by picking up the ingredients by hand and lightly tossing in the air and letting them fall back in the bowl. Repeat several times until well blended.

2. Add warm water slowly, while mixing with hands or fork until dough is formed.

3. Knead the dough with hands for about three minutes until the dough is soft and elastic in texture.

4. Cover dough with a dishcloth and let it rise five to fifteen minutes.

5. In a cast iron frying pan, heat lard or shortening. This oil needs to be deep enough for bread to float when it is cooking. (An electric frying pan can be used.) To see if the oil is hot enough, sprinkle with just a drop of water. If it sizzles, it is ready for frying.

Forming the Bread Loaves

1. Pinch off a ball of the dough with your hands, about two inches (5.08 cm) in diameter.

2. Flatten and stretch with your hands and slap back and forth from hand to hand. Repeat this process until it looks like the size of a salad plate (about six inches [15.24 cm] in diameter).

GA1322

Cooking the Fry Bread

1. Carefully take the flattened dough and put it in the HOT shortening. Fry until it is yellow-brown on one side and then carefully turn over. A cooking fork or long stick can be used to turn the bread over. (This process should be closely supervised by an adult.)

2. When bread is a golden yellow-brown, lift it out of the pan and hold it over the pan just for a few seconds to let the excess oil drip in the pan. Remove and stack.

Fry bread can be served with honey, sprinkled with salt or cinnamon sugar. It is frequently eaten with meals and can also be used as a base for what is called Indian tacos.

Indian Tacos

An Indian taco is very much like a Mexican tostada and is a meal in itself. These are often made in restaurants and homes in the Southwest.

Prepare the following:

    1 head of lettuce, shredded (2 cups [480 ml])
    2 medium tomatoes, diced
    2 medium onions, diced
    1 pound (.45 kg) cheddar cheese, shredded
    4-6 cups (960-1440 ml) cooked pinto beans

Prepare the ingredients and make the fry bread. Prepare the taco as described below.

Place the prepared ingredients in layers on the fry bread in the following order: cooked beans, onions, tomatoes, lettuce and cheese.

Add chili or salsa if desired on top and enjoy!

Roasted Fresh Corn

Corn can be roasted in a hole in the ground. Since this may not be easily done on most school grounds, you might try roasting ears of corn on a barbecue (leaving the husks attached).

You will need fresh ears of corn with husks, a barbecue pit, charcoal or firewood, long tongs and bowls or platters for the cooked corn.

When the coals are red and hot, place the ears of corn on the grill. Leave them to cook. Turn every so often to make sure the corn is being cooked on all sides. When done and ready to eat, pull back the cornhusks. If you leave the husks attached, they can be used as a natural handle to hold the corn while eating.

Other Activities

Earlier we talked about family cultures. In your own homes there are probably many special foods that you and your family may enjoy eating. What are some of those foods? Where did the foods originate? Talk about them in class. The following activities may be interesting to do, as well as fun and delicious.

1. Have a traditional food sharing day. Each person in the class brings one favorite traditional dish of food that can be shared with friends in the classroom.

2. On different days each person in the class shares a cooking experience of one family favorite cultural food item. You might even choose to have someone from your family come to the class and demonstrate how this food is prepared. The class could also be involved with the cooking process. Make sure that enough food is being prepared so that everyone has an opportunity to taste.

3. Make a class cookbook. Draw a picture of your favorite food and write the recipe below the picture. The teacher can then gather all the recipes and make copies. The cookbook is now ready to be put together. Enough copies should be made so that each student will have his own classroom cookbook to share with his/her family. It might also be nice to mention where the recipes came from. You may have a recipe similar to a friend's and that is okay. They should all be included in the book.

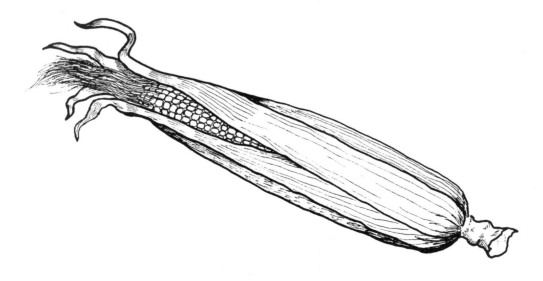

GA1322

Researching Bread

Many cultures have some type of bread that is either prepared daily or for special celebrations.

1. For many Native American Indians, fry bread is traditional and common. See if you can find other cultures that have a similar kind of bread in their own traditions. Report on those similar kinds of breads and the cultures they come from.

2. Since fry bread is like a fried tortilla, maybe you would like to find out what cultures have tortilla-like bread. See what you can come up with. How are the breads alike and how are they different?

3. Have a bread tasting party. In groups, gather different kinds of breads from different cultures. There might even be several cultural bakeries in your area, like French bakeries, bagel shops, tortilla shop, etc., from which you can purchase or ask for samples to bring to class. Display the breads on a table and label what cultures they come from. Then enjoy tasting.

4. If there are different cultural bakeries in your area, you might want to ask the owners to explain about the breads and if there are special kinds of food that these breads are eaten with or special celebrations that they are traditionally made for.

5. After studying the different kinds of breads in the world, take small pieces of paper and write down the names of the breads and tape or pin the names on the areas where the breads come from. A globe or a large world map will be helpful with this activity.

Researching Your Environment for Natural Foods

Remember that years ago the Native American Indian people lived on what was available on the land that provided nutrition. If you were living in the forest or mountains in and around where you now live, what kinds of natural foods would be available for you to survive on? Make a listing of those foods and the areas in which they can be found.

Researching Culturally Traditional Foods

If you are fortunate to have a variety of cultures in the area where you live and go to school, it certainly would be interesting to research the cultures that are in your community and the goods of those cultures. You might even choose to visit any restaurants that have these foods or invite the owners of those restaurants to talk to the class about the foods that are prepared and maybe demonstrate the preparation of a particular dish you are interested in learning how to make.

Researching Corn

Since corn is used in many cultures, you might want to find out where it originated, how it has developed over the years and how it was transported to different countries.

There might be other kinds of foods that you would like to find more information about. What food items are you interested in learning about?

Teacher Resources

Children's Book List

Anne and the Old One
Arrow to the Sun: A Pueblo Indian Tale
Gerald McDermott, author and artist
Viking Press
625 Madison Ave.
New York 10022
Copyright 1974

Circle of Life: The Miccosukee Indian Way
Authors: Nancy Hendersen and Jane Dewey

The Friendly Wolf
Paul Globe, author and artist
Bradbury Press
2 Overhill Road
Scarsdale, NY 10583

The Girl Who Loved Wild Horses
Paul Globe, author and artist
Bradbury Press
2 Overhill Road
Scarsdale, NY 10583
Copyright 1978

Hawk, I'm Your Brother
B. Baylor
Scribner's
New York
Copyright 1976

*Interviews with Native American Men and Women
in Various Jobs*
United Indians of All Tribes Foundation
Copyright 1980

Kevin Cloud: Chippewa Boy in the City
CA Bales
Reilly & Lee
Chicago, IL
Copyright 1972

Knots on a Counting Rope
Bill Martin, Jr., and John Archambault
Illustrated by Ted Rand
Published by The Trumpet Club, a Division of Bantam
Doubleday Dell Publishing Group, Inc.
666 Fifth Ave.
New York, NY 10103
Copyright 1966/1987

The Legend of the Bluebonnet
T. de Paola
Putnam
New York
Copyright 1983

Nashdoi Yaazh Bil hazaadi nooyeel
(Navajo—book about mountain lions)
Native American Material Development Center
National Geographic Society
Copyright 1972

Red Ribbons for Emma
New Mexico People and Energy Collective
New Seeds Press
Berkeley, CA
Copyright 1981

Sharing Our Worlds: Native American Children Today
United Indians of All Tribes Foundation
Copyright 1979

A Salmon for Simon
B. Waterton
Douglas & McIntyre
Salem House
462 Boston St.
Topsfield, MA 01983
Copyright 1978

Spider Woman
A. Cameron
Harbour Publishing Co.
Maderia Park, BC
Copyright 1988

Stephanie and the Coyote
J Crowder
Upper Strata
Box 278
Bernallio, NM 87004
Copyright 1969

Films

Contrary Warriors, a documentary film about the Crow people
Department of Library Services
Narration: Peter Coyote
Rattlesnake Productions, Inc.

Dances with Wolves PG13
Produced and directed by Kevin Costner
An ORION pictures release

There are two excellent books that can be used for addressing the issue of stereotypes and antibiased curricula. You will find these resources full of curriculum ideas that will add to and enhance teaching children about Native American Indians.

Unlearning Indian Stereotypes: A Teaching Unit for Elementary Teachers and Children's Librarians, published by The Racism and Sexism Resource Center for Educators, a Division of the Council on Interracial Books for Children. Copyright 1977.

Anti-Bias Curriculum: Tools for Empowering Young Children, Louise Derman-Sparks and the ABC Task Force, published by the National Association for the Education of Young Children, 1834 Connecticut Ave, N.W., Washington, D.C. 20009-5786. Library Congress Catalog Card Number: 88-063731. Copyright 1989.

Other Resources

American Indian Resource Center
Huntington Park Library
6518 Miles Ave.
Huntington Park, CA 90255
213-583-1461

Navajo Curriculum Center Press
Rough Rock Demonstration School
P.O. Box 217
Chinle, AZ 86503
602-728-3311

Claudia's Caravan
P.O. Box 1582
Alameda, CA 94501
415-521-7871

United Indians of All Tribes Foundation
P.O. Box 99100
Seattle, WA 98199
206-285-4425

Council on Interracial Books for Children
1841 Broadway
New York, NY 10023
212-757-5339

GA1322